NANNY AND I

NANNY AND I

Ruth Plant

WILLIAM KIMBER · LONDON

First published in 1978 by
WILLIAM KIMBER & CO. LIMITED
Godolphin House,
22a Queen Anne's Gate,
London, SW1H 9AE

© Ruth Plant, 1978

ISBN 0 7183 0495 0

Photoset in Great Britain by
Specialised Offset Services Limited, Liverpool
and printed by
REDWOOD BURN LIMITED
Trowbridge and Esher

Contents

List of Illustrations

This was given to me by my Nanny, Agnes Jones, who said she felt it should be her epitaph!

Though she never knew I would write this book about her.

I

My First Sortie

I began to walk in the long, hot summer of 1911, the last, perhaps, in which thinking people could bask in the sun in tranquillity, for the years ahead were to be full of fear, and the later ones of ghostly memories.

It must be an important experience to make one's first vertical contact with the earth, and to know the delights of locomotion. But few, if any, conscious memories of this event seem to remain with us. I myself can just recall a bright red garment and a sloping lawn, both of which, my mother told me, I used in my first independent sorties into the world.

It was the year we took Sandon vicarage. My father was an Anglican clergyman and in those days, when stipends were poor, and holiday facilities too few, it was the regular custom to arrange these temporary exchanges, each locum hoping that as few of his new flock as possible would fall ill or marry, each wife hoping the cook-general would fit happily into yet another rambling house, the labyrinths of which were new to her. It was not a vast change in the domestic horizon. Usually, it only meant moving from one sunless dwelling to another, the light constricted by the same nineteenth century perpendicular tracery, the design of which Eric Gill – then a young architect – came out of the Ecclesiastical Commissioners in protest against at this time.

It was, perhaps, an attempt to bring colour to this stereotyped environment that made one vicar put an advertisement in a Church newspaper which ran: 'Holiday exchange. Lovely old world vicarage, with two packs of hounds constantly passing through.'

My father delighted to quote this, remarking that it was such a fitting analogy of our home on a busy parochial morning.

A year later we took Hixon, another typical vicarage in the same part of Staffordshire. It stood on a hill, with a steep drive flanked by rhododendrons and a large wooden gate, to admit carriages. There seemed nothing remarkable or ominous about this slightly dingy dwelling, but it was here that so much of importance in world history was to make its impact on us.

Normally the winds of change scarcely touched us, for we not only had two parents of whom we were extremely fond, but also that strange English institution, a perfect nanny. She came from the kinder more pastoral part of the county, the Shropshire borders, and it seemed only appropriate that she was the daughter of the village carpenter. She was not the fierce ordering type, but essentially gentle. I don't think for this reason that she ever spoilt us by bribes and sweets in order to obtain good behaviour like some more conventionally organised nannies have been known to do. When she criticised or gave advice it was in a slow, thoughtful manner and her voice was more pleading than angry.

That this gained our respect seems to be illustrated by an episode one night in the bathroom when my brother, having been put entirely into clean clothes, including a clean dressing gown, insisted on sitting on the bath edge while she was dressing me. She warned him that his position was precarious, but he laughed at the idea. Then, suddenly, there was a shriek and a splash, and he fell backwards into the water, being soaked from head to foot.

When he was pulled out, his carefully washed clothes a soaking mess, I do not recall that there were any bitter recriminations from Nanny, but that Ralph with great dignity for his slender years stood up and said, 'Well, Nanny, you are a cleverer woman than I thought you.' A remark that became famous in the family history.

The life of a child in the earlier years of this century differed tremendously according to its social station. There was no Welfare State and clinics for mothers with babies to obtain advice and training from. There was a high mortality rate among the poorer families though we lived in a country village, while children of parents even with the modest financial resources of the Vicar received infinite care. Those were such leisurely days in a quiet rural place, there was little to disturb the domestic routine, as one of Nanny's earlier letters to my mother shows.

It also shows what an indispensable person Nanny was, not a remote dominating figure ruling in the nursery sphere but a friend of the whole family, willing to turn her hand to anything and make up for the deficiencies of the young maid, all we could afford to keep in the kitchen at that time.

Dear Mistress,

Sunday night 7.30 Babe is in a beautiful sleep. I have just been down and put Master's supper all ready for Alice to carry in as soon as he comes from Church. I ordered $2\frac{1}{2}$ lbs of steak. We have got a nice bit of mutton left yet but I cooked the steak for the Master tonight as I thought he may be getting tired of the mutton and it would be nice for him to have something fresh. I got Alice to do some beans for him, there was a nice bit of suet with the steak so I cut it off and have made him a little ginger pudding steamed. It has turned out so nice and light.

Thank you very much for your letter of this morning. Babe was so pleased with his post card and more so to hear about the rock, he sat up in bed and clapped his little hands with such delight and wanted to know if it was tomorrow you were bringing it. We have had a very nice day together and baby has been such a dear, happy little laddie. I had him out in the garden a bit this morning and after dinner we went into Mr Shelley's cornfield and through the turnips up to that wood. Babe did so enjoy his little self I had to wait at the side of the bank while he kept running under the trees for some fir cones, we got quite a nice lot and as we came back he dragged some of the sheaves of oats to another stack and made a little cubby house he said. Today he said, 'What's for me dinner, Nan?' When I told him an egg he said, 'Oh gracious if you don't give me more than an egg I shall faint for food.'

He is looking so well and bonny and I do so hope he will keep like this until you get back and for a long time. He is eating so well. The walk in an afternoon seems to do baby a lot of good. Yesterday and today he came back and had a very tea and seemed to really enjoy it. I have not altered his petticoat although the weather is much warmer than it was. I don't think this thick petticoat is much warmer than the other two together only perhaps the sleeves, and the old Jaeger ones are so very small on him now.

I took a blanket out of the 'Tommer room' on Friday as I thought we could do with one and Babe has slept better these last two nights for it. Alice is getting along very well on the whole. Her bit of work lasts her all day, the 'keer' moods as baby says come on occasionally. I think it must have been the tea that day. She's a funny girl when you know her, quite different to what I thought she would be.

The Master has asked me to send you Miss Nuttall's letter [Aunt Nellie] so I will look for a larger envelope. Baby is getting shocking for cutting things. Today he managed to get hold of the scissors and was very quiet behind me, I turned round to see what he was up to. He started to dance, looked so mischievous and said, 'Oh Nan, you don't know what I've done, look.' He had only taken a piece out of my blouse, also a piece out of his own sock, a good thing they were not his last new ones. He is pulling all those balls off the curtains on the landing, there are only five on the floor I can see now, he likes to kick them and make them roll along.

The Master asked Alice to put his bag ready. I did as she did not know what to put in. I hope I remembered all he would want.

When my mother was away Nanny took over all her responsibilities including the cooking, which was very good of her.

My brother adored Nanny and it was perhaps interesting to note as a background to this, that Mummy used to laugh and say the only time that Nanny was really rude to her in all their years together was when my mother broke the news to her that I was expected. 'A second baby? Well!' she said indignantly. 'It's very hard on the boy.'

My brother was so fond of her that one day when a visiting parson's wife spending the day with us, ventured to put her baby to rest on Nanny's bed and roll it in Nanny's dressing gown which she happened to see hanging on the door, Ralph took hold of the garment in fury and tugged it free, nearly rolling the baby onto the floor!

In spite of this devotion, however, which started five years before I was born I never felt left out or the second best in her affections. Once I was there she seemed to express such abundant affection for her charges that I became just as much loved as Ralph; in fact it was she who defended me against his brotherly cruelties of teasing and telling me alarming tales. I recall on one occasion that she found me in great distress because Ralph had just told me that my navel was a screw that held together the whole of my body and if he or anyone turned it I should drop into little pieces all over the floor!

Nanny was able to refute these stories firmly; that was, all except one he told me at Hixon Vicarage in 1914 that last summer we were there which caused a whole landslide in my sense of security. But life was much the same there, at first at any rate, for my brother and me. Our peaceful exploration of local lanes with Nanny continued, but over a new area, of course. There was the added interest of a level crossing, where we could watch the trains, and a new village store where they kept a particularly potent brand of lemonkali. This was of a dangerous bromide shade, and the major explosion of fizzy bitterness that it produced in the mouth made its consumption an experience to revel in.

In those days we were quite unversed in the real bitterness of this barbaric world. We had our private sorrows and terrors, of course, but the happiness and security of our home life formed a solid background to everything. Events that happened beyond the family circle had up till now seemed of little importance, and certainly caused no alarm. The first invasion of excitement from the outside world, however (and the heralding of a new age, had we but known it) came when the Manchester to London Air Race was planned over Hixon. My brother, who was already a model aeroplane enthusiast, was overjoyed when he found that we had taken a house 'on the course'. I think we all became caught up in his enthusiasm.

A highly organised programme was planned for the great day, almost the equivalent of a military exercise. Breakfast was to be served early and, weather permitting, other meals were to be taken out of doors. Field glasses were to be ready, to avoid missing a moment of the show. To those of us who had never seen anything bigger than a toy aeroplane in flight, the prospect of seeing many huge machines passing over us laden with human beings was exciting in the extreme.

Everything would have gone beautifully, had not Blériot (who was afterwards to become famous as the first aviator to cross the Channel) decided to fly over the course the day before. I do not know who first heard the incredible sound of the approaching giant, and gave the alarm. Probably it was my brother, but in a few moments the entire household was in a state of chaos, nearing panic. Everybody's idea was to get out of the house to see the monster, and so they all made for the front door at once. My mother's experience was the most unfortunate, as she decided to go through it at exactly the same moment as Mrs Cash, the cook, the latter having in her excitement entirely overlooked the rigid custom observed in those days of precedence for employers in doorways. This caused a head-on collision. As Mrs Cash was the fat, traditional kind of cook, my mother came off decidedly the worst in the encounter.

We must have overcome this delaying action, however, for I recall running wildly across the lawn with my mother and Nanny beside me, and then being lifted over the wooden palings into the paddock. From here, to our satisfaction, we gained a grassy knoll, beyond the trees which had obscured our view in the garden. My brother had long ago arrived there, and was calmly focussing the field glasses on the clattering monster which was fast approaching.

All seemed satisfactorily achieved until suddenly my mother, with her concern for wrapping up common to the mothers of those days, cried: 'Oh, Ruth hasn't got her coat on! She will catch such a cold!'

This cry went straight to the heart of my Nanny, who was indeed a treasure even in those exacting days. In the same self-sacrificing spirit which makes a servant defend his master even in the face of a pack of attacking wolves, Nanny set off to the house to fetch it.

Arriving there, with great rapidity as she told us afterwards, she seized up the coat in the hall, gained the doorway safely and crossed the lawn with the engines still roaring overhead. But like a would-be Grand National winner, she tired the second time round the course, and fell heavily at the last fence. She often described her feelings when attempting to pull herself over the paddock palings, she fell headlong into a bed of nettles, only extricating herself as the buzz of the engine died away.

It seems a long way from that exciting scramble for the vicarage paddock with the primitive engine clattering overhead, to the neatly docketed 'channels' of London Airport, the floating elegance of the great machines waiting on the runways. The sophisticated crowds who file through each appointed doorway have the detachment of a robot world. Whether they merely cross the Alps for a fortnight's skiing, or cover the hard-won route over the Atlantic, their faces show no emotion, no appreciation of the hazardous struggles of the pioneers who opened the route.

Will it still be the same if, in a few short years, we arrive at the airport and hear the honeyed voice of the announcer say: 'British Outer Space Airways announce the departure of their Flight 207 to the moon'? Shall we never again capture the thrill of wonder and excitement on that summer afternoon in a vicarage paddock when we were all 'children' together in the aviation world?

II

Life at the Vicarage

It was usually a wet day when we returned from our holiday to our permanent home, a large vicarage in the northern part of the county. On that late August day, it always seemed as if summer had completely ended.

Nanny, coming from the kinder atmosphere of the Shropshire border, readily joined my mother in her lamentations of the summer gone by and began the ritual of putting away our summer clothes, such dignified, starched affairs in those days, sharply divided from the warm ones we wore in winter.

I do not think we children minded which season it was, we were engrossed and satisfied by the surroundings of our home. There were in those days no visual aids to education, and although this no doubt narrowed our horizon, it certainly increased our imagination and awareness of things immediately round us. In that big house and garden, there were so many things to see and enjoy that might have seemed commonplace to the outside world, but to us they were like personal friends and were always a source of entertainment.

My most pleasurable memory is of waking up in the nursery in the joyous anticipation of the day's activities. The room faced south, and the wall outside was covered with wistaria. Perhaps it is because of this that the flower is always such a special delight to me. In the early summer it hung from the walls in great mauvy blue festoons, and later on when the flowers had fallen the twisted woody stems were covered with nasturtiums climbing upward in colourful disorderliness.

Because of this procession of flowers through the summer, myriads of bees came to bask on them in the cosy warmth of the wall. Their soothing, leisurely chorus stole in on my awakening senses like background music. To me, they became the personification of peace and security as I lay, lazily watching the shiny green blind flapping in the breeze, letting intermittent shafts of sunlight into the darkened room, and thinking gloatingly of the sunny day waiting to be enjoyed outside.

It was on the lawn below the window that my father used to exercise the beagle families in spring. The puppies, grotesque, wrinkle-faced creatures, swaying drunkenly about on their flabby legs while the mother in her delight at being free would tear round the lawn wildly, her long ears flying back like a maiden's hair, a twinkle in her deep, brown eyes. As she ran, she would narrow the circle gradually inwards until she came within reach of her progeny. Then she would give one of them a mischievous push with her nose as she passed, sending the fat little bundle rolling over squeakily on the daisy-covered lawn. After this she would fly on, her eyes smiling with amusement, zigzagging hither and thither in joyous abandonment.

As there were no hares in our neighbourhood, the question of hunting with the beagles did not come to the fore. It was only later that I came to realise how man diabolically channels this mischievous love of speed and chase into the pursuit and brutal destruction of one of the most lovely and sensitive creatures in the animal world.

We had to be careful not to let two beagles out at a time because if we did they would run up to each other, touch noses and make some surreptitious agreement to go out hunting on their own, chasing, but never catching rabbits. They seem to have no blood lust but a passion for scent. They would sometimes even meet the rabbits coming out of the wood and pass them by with noses glued to the ground.

We never had any complaints from farmers about them chasing sheep but when the corn was getting up there was a danger they would lay it through making tunnels into the crop, following a rabbit scent.

My father's beagles were well known in the parish. In those days it was reasonably safe for a dog to wander around. My father was in the habit of taking one or other of them parish visiting, but if the visit proved long and they got bored waiting outside they would go round to the back to inspect the dustbins. Like so many hounds, how ever well they were fed they seemed to retain this delight in foraging. If the Kennel Club kept their records in the form of a dogs' *Who's Who* I am sure that many of them would put down 'Interest in dustbins' under the heading 'Recreation'.

Owing to pre-occupation with some stale culinary delicacy or other object of curiosity they would fail to realise that my father was leaving and moving on to another house and would wait there with dog-like devotion until some junior member of the house or a neighbour searched out a piece of rough string and brought the highly co-operative 'stray' back to its home. Of course such concern for the animal could not go unrewarded, and generally a shilling was meted out in reward. After the habit got known around the village, however, the frequency with which the beagles apparently got 'lost' and were brought home, became a little embarrassing and sometimes I am afraid they were apprehended on their independent and lawful journeys, by small boys requiring pocket money.

Such sorties did stand them in good stead sometimes. There was Boaster, for instance, a particularly large and lazy hound of a somewhat greedy nature who used to make the quite considerable journey up to the middle of the village and down Sarver Lane to a ghastly offal heap composed of entrails flung out from the local slaughter house. One day, returning from one of these expeditions, he did not bother to make it to the Vicarage, but lay down in the sun for an after lunch nap outside The Miners Arms, the pub just between the Vicarage and the Church.

The story goes that the driver of a horse-drawn dray, who had lunched rather adequately on the local beer, came out of the pub and in his foggy state never noticed the dog and drove straight over him. But Boaster was not in the least injured by this. The only way my father could account for his miraculous escape was that he had filled his stomach so full of offal it was somehow padded.

When he went to shows he was entered under his proper name which was Weston Cyprus – Weston because he was bred at Weston-on-Trent, my grandfather's home, but why

Cyprus I have quite forgotten. At one show, however, they misread the name on the entry form and he was seen sitting proudly under a label 'Western Express'. There was no hound less like an express but no passer-by at the show knew that.

My father also bred a hound called Bashful, who actually had far more reason to boast because she became the champion of England. As he could not afford to do a lot of showing he sold her to Mrs Peter Robinson, but when Bashful grew old bought her back to enjoy a peaceful retirement in her old home. Alas, she was not as lucky as Boaster. She did not have long with us. She was heard to cry out in the road one day when a bicycle passed, and then ran into the garden spitting blood and died soon after, having been fatally injured, we thought, in some way by its wheels.

My father's fame in beagle breeding linked him up with many interesting people, and there was great excitement when the Marquis of Lintithgow decided to come to lunch. He arrived in a car which was very much the rich man's prerogative in those days. A crisis nearly occurred when he expressed a desire to have his brandy flask fetched, his chauffeur, apparently, being custodian of it. Perhaps our modest financial position did not permit us to include this connoisseur's drink on the menu. If my father drank at all he had a whisky and soda.

Nanny, who was as usual I suppose playing the part of parlourmaid for a special occasion, was sent out to get it. So tensed up was she about being entrusted with the belongings of a marquis that she failed to grasp it properly when the chauffeur handed it to her. Luckily, as custodian of this important article in his master's entourage, he quickly realised what was happening, grabbed it, Nanny grabbed it, and then they almost dropped it again between them.

It was a longstanding family joke how Nanny played pitch and toss with the marquis's brandy flask! Somehow combined efforts enabled it to reach the marquis intact and the lunch party passed off as a great success.

The lawn where the beagles played was surrounded by shrubs, the inevitable rhododendron clumps on one side sloping upwards towards the yard. On the other side was a large, mixed shrubbery, almost amounting to a spinney, which was dominated by three enormous ash trees. To me they seemed the very tallest trees you could ever see, with their thin, green trunks, covered with a soft bloom, stretching upwards almost beyond my sight.

When the days grew longer after Christmas, and the winter sunshine took on the brighter colouring at the edge of spring, I used to watch them casting long, naked shadows across the lawn, and feel that this was inexplicitly a sign that summer was really on the way.

At the end of the lawn was a gigantic 'Christmas' tree with feathery arms outstretched nearly to the ground. When you ascended the grassy bank on which it grew and stood underneath it peering upwards, you could see a world of dark branches with small fir cones hanging from them. The ground beneath was a mass of cones too and prickly needles. You could run your fingers deliciously through them piling them up into strange heaps and furrows according to taste.

Beside the tree in some grassier ground we buried our two pet rabbits killed, I regret to say, by the rats who broke into their pen. The only choral items we had for the funeral were 'While Shepherds watched' and 'Come all ye faithful' played on an old fashioned gramophone with a huge tomato coloured horn, like a giant gloxinia. It must have looked rather striking under the dark fir tree, but we did not notice this, nor the irrelevancy of the choral items so absorbed were we with the solemnity of the occasion.

At the side of the tree there was a gate and a fence made of hurdles, and through this you passed into the back drive and thence to the paddock, through a wicket gate of wood, an entrance dominated by a magnificent walnut tree, from a branch of which a swing hung. On this you could fly upwards into its branches watching their fascinating symmetry and almost touching a bouquet of mistletoe which sprouted out high above. I don't know if hurdles were very expensive and that is why chestnut fencing has inevitably replaced them, but they make me feel nostalgic for well kept parklands with vast trees and grazing horses and a glimpse of velvet lawns. Hurdles were the first steps on the ladder of social qualification for a country house of importance in those days. Although I personally found only alarm and often boredom in such formal social surroundings, I cannot help having an artistic longing for this sight which symbolises to me peace and security.

I still have a picture of Nanny, myself and my brother standing by the gate into the paddock. The branches of the walnut tree hang down behind us almost like those of a tropical palm. Beyond it you can just glimpse the roof of the kennels and the railings of the run where Daddy used to house his beagles when they had puppies. Nanny is in a strangely abundant white apron and blue print, with a starched cap piled on her pretty hair. My brother, though only about five years old, is already clad in a heavy overcoat and thick black wool stockings and a manly cap. I myself, being a babe in arms, am swathed in shawls topped by a large bonnet edged with what resembles an enormous cake frill, from which naturally uncomfortable surroundings I am peering out disapprovingly at the world.

The paddock, when I reached a stage capable of mobility, was one of my greatest joys in summer. I shall never forget the experience of walking through waist high buttercups on early June mornings when the sunlight touched them so vividly, they seemed to radiate back something which was more glittering even than real gold. As it was our own crop no one seemed to mind my making a pathway across it at the thickest part and here I could, being not very old and tall, wander on at will encompassed by an entire forest of gold. It always seems that buttercups now are very scarce and never so high and abundant as they were in those elysian days.

At the bottom of the drive round a sharp bend the backyard began. A huge stretch of cobblestone flanked on the left by enormous rhododendron bushes shielding the house and the lawn from it. On the right hand side there was a long line of outhouses. 'Sixty yards of buildings,' my mother used to say wearily, 'and all our own dilapidations to do.' A previous incumbent Parson Dawes had farmed his own glebe and this was the legacy he had left to his successors.

The first building was the dog house where most of the beagles were kept. As my father bred them for showing, sometimes he had as many as fifteen at once. I remember my delight at peeping over the half-length door which penned them in in daytime, and seeing them all sitting there unconscious of my presence. Sometimes an apprehensive hound would raise his head and bay at this sudden intrusion of a pair of eyes just above the top of the door but on seeing my amusement and realising my identity he would stop sheepishly and wag his tail. Then they would all rush to the door delightedly to lick my hand.

Next to the dog house was 'the boys' room' – why so called I never discovered. I think some years before some of the village lads had used my father's carpentry bench there, the beginnings of a boys' club I suppose. Nobody talked of such things as boys' clubs in those days, though I suppose there were pioneer efforts already going in the slums.

After this came the coach house, a vast place planned no doubt to house a full-sized family coach in the old days when Parson Dawes lived there farming affluently. In our day it only housed one small governess cart.

Next to the coach house was the stable, also a vast place with stalls for several horses. We only kept one little Russian pony there called Merrylegs, and later Jinnie the donkey. Merrylegs was left free in a large stall on the left of the door enclosed with slotted rails across the entrance. Her hooves made an exciting clatter on the brick floor as she swung round quickly to greet you when you entered. She was very friendly and docile, but whenever we were going out our old gardener would harness her at least half an hour beforehand and stand firmly at her head under the misguided impression that she might bolt at any minute (though my mother was inclined to think he enjoyed an easy morning this way). Actually, Merrylegs, in spite of her name, never went at more than a gentle trot, though it was generally noticed that she somewhat accelerated when her head was turned towards home.

It was a very pleasant form of locomotion travelling in a governess cart, especially on a lovely summer day. You were so closely in touch with the beauties of your surroundings. If you put out your hand you could stroke the flowers as the cart passed slowly along the narrow lanes, and their perfume was wafted up in waves from the warm banks on either side.

There was an individual style and personality about a pony which motor cars seldom have. No horse was ever called

Austin A 40 or Morris 1000 and you did not see dozens of similar models coming down the road to meet you. Each animal and accompanying 'turnout' was individual and seemed to fit the personality of its owner.

At the Vicarage, for instance, we had our practical little brown creature, Merrylegs with her rough coat, hardy for going out in all weathers, harnessed to a solid brown governess cart, tough enough to jolt over the stones of any parochial byways.

Our squiress on the other hand, owned a smart clipped animal of pure white called Snowball. Her governess cart had elegant dashboards and cream spokes to the wheels, which were beautifully kept by an attentive groom. Snowball did not jog along like Merrylegs but moved in a rather sophisticated high-stepping style. She was a picturesque sight when she trotted by with the family, usually in rather large hats, sitting upright in the trap, accompanied by several dogs, as passengers, who were sitting on the seat their noses in the air, either in pursuit of wafting sniffs of rabbit or social grandeur, I could never decide which.

In later years when the cost of living went up we had regretfully to give Merrylegs up. We found her a good home with a farmer who was a special friend of ours. He was very kind to her for the rest of her life but it was always a great sorrow to us that at the end he sent her away to be killed at a knacker's yard. We knew nothing of the conventional arrangements for disposing of worn out horses then. We thought he would shoot her himself at the farm. If only we had known we would have arranged for a vet to come and destroy her as a sick animal on the farm. But since I have come to believe in the survival of *loved* animals and that in their new bodies in the after life they can communicate with us by thought, I am looking forward to meeting her one day and apologising for our omission, and driving out once again in the pony cart to the sound of her jangling bell in a world of perpetually sunlit lanes, where there is no knacker's yard at the end of the journey.

Next to the stable was a place we called the coal cellar, because we kept the coal there, though it was obvious from the mangers inside it that it had once been Parson Dawes' cowshed. The windows had been closed up making it into a sort of Black Hole of Calcutta. It was inside this place that I learnt a piece of the truth that was to affect my whole life.

We had a pet cockerel called Harry of the grey Plymouth Rock variety fashionable in those days. He came out of a hen's egg that one of my pet bantams had hatched out for some reason and he was a bit of an odd man out. It was suggested therefore one day that as he was superfluous Nanny should catch Harry and a man would call and take him to market. I agreed to this because I did not then realise that it was in reality to his death. Nanny explained that I would not like to help her catch Harry, but I felt I should try to be like other people and take things of this kind as a part of normal life. So although my instinct was against it I decided to help.

I remember that after an agonising chase round the yard she finally cornered the shrieking Harry in that black inferno the coal cellar. By then I could no longer countenance this appalling treachery to a friend and ran to Nanny begging her to let him go. But she thrust him into a big tub with a lid on that stood there somewhere in the dark, saying that a man would soon call and take him to market. She also added, I remember, that I should not have helped as she had said it would not be nice.

Nanny's solution did not satisfy me, however; merely to turn one's back on something like this because it was not nice did not solve the problem. Suddenly I saw the objective truth. Why should Harry who had learnt to trust us and looked to us for food and subsistence for his life be suddenly attacked like this viciously and hounded to his death. Wasn't it a piece of blatant barbarism on our part, who were the so-called civilised occupants of the world? What stupid phrases like 'chicken is so delicious' had been built up over the years to pad the corners of reality for the stupid and make them accept these daily massacres.

I saw it all then in a flash with the simple logic of a child's mind, yet it took me twenty years to overcome the social convention surrounding the practice of meat eating and take the really positive action of giving up eating any creature that has lived or felt.

III

The Enclosing Garden

Down a small winding path out of the yard, edged with ferns and syringa bushes planted on an encampment of rocks, you entered the kitchen garden. The way was deliciously scented, first with the damp smell of rocks and ferns, and then with the fragrance of old fashioned moss roses and box trees that grew just inside the garden. This was the garden I loved best, for it was not just a plot full of vegetables, but a place of infinite variety and character safely enclosed against disturbances or scrutiny of the outside world.

On the north side there was a double hedge with a large space in between which afforded us a gloriously secluded enclosure for our 'Cubby House'. My brother built it out of sacks, held up by bamboo sticks. It provided quite convincingly the impression of four sheltering walls. I surreptitiously took some china out there from the kitchen and felt a residential pride akin to the delights of having a flat of one's own in town I suppose. It must have been in the autumn that we built this famous erection for I connect it with dry swept leaves and the smell of them burning in the clear autumn air.

In the garden itself, sheltered by the double hedge which bent round in a curve, were a cluster of little diamond shaped beds edged with clipped ivy. Here Nanny's precious autumn crocuses grew. They were a wonderful glowing mauve, much bigger than the spring ones and were memorable because they came out at such an unusual time. Nanny had brought them all the way from her home on the Shropshire borders and we considered them something very special.

The crown of the kitchen garden was the herbaceous border which came next, standing on the top of a rise. It was here that

I learnt to love the beauty of deep blue delphiniums and lupins mixed with the red of poppies and old-fashioned peonies. How glorious their colours seemed to be then.

Along the top of the garden sheltered by the thick hedge the herbs were planted. We had far more in those days. Camomile which Nanny made into tea if we were bilious and trees of 'Old Man', a herb which gave off a sharp smell if you rubbed it in between your fingers. The scent of thyme drifted up from the warm soil deliciously as one walked along the crunching gravel path.

In the middle of the garden were large areas of vegetables impersonal and fluctuating, not of great interest to me, but there were some landmarks like the artichoke bed which seemed to me at that age like a tropical bamboo forest, fascinating tall stems growing at random all over the ground assigned to them.

The rhubarb bed too was a memorable spot because its earth did not only contain the conventional red sticks of fruit and the bottomless buckets turned upside down for forcing – the fore-runner of the cloche I suppose – but also a strange collection of bones and odd gloves and other paraphernalia brought there by the beagles. Immediately they picked up such exciting objects, and it was disturbing how constantly the family gloves disappeared, they proceeded hastily to the rhubarb bed and drove their treasure safe into the earth, covering it up laboriously with their noses, their long ears getting impregnated with soil. I remember seeing a beagle dart at one of the cats in an absentminded moment when she met one there. Then she checked herself, suddenly realising this was a breach of normal good neighbourliness, and a risky proceeding since the hounds were always very much in awe of the cats. Then she waited agonisedly while the cat indolently picked its way over the exact piece of soil that had been recently pushed over some treasure. When the elegant creature had swept on the beagle returned and gave the earth a few more emphatic nudges with her nose as if to protect it against any future trespass.

In the far corner of the garden was the paraffin house, a strange edifice with a sharply pointed roof, the whole thing built of corrugated iron. It nestled in a clump of bushes which prevented it being too much of an eyesore. In its dark and smelly interior one could see a fifty gallon cask placed on a stand rather like a huge barrel of beer. The smell was very potent and the floor was covered with beetles, great black creatures reflecting blue lights from their shiny shells. Many appeared to die from the effects of paraffin. They lay on their backs their thin spidery legs pointing upwards. From this mysterious cavern of disturbing sights and smells one crept away alarmed yet fascinated.

Behind this sinister shed, right at the end of the garden, stood the sycamore tree, a kind of outpost stretching out into the ordinary world. It was from here that I used to observe the goings on, quietly and with detachment, for I knew that the foundations of my own world rested firmly on the cornerstone of a happy home.

The tree stood on a small bank and reached far above the road. You could scramble up it from some bushes at the back and sit in a cleft where the trunk divided in two and watch the passers by. There were mysterious strangers to wonder about, followed by familiar parish figures, who passed by deep in thought, sometimes giving vent to a mumbled word or gesture. Then there was the cowman who came night and morning, driving the herd in to be milked. I felt a thrill of security as the little red bull skirmished about in the road and the excited collie ran to and fro at its heels. Had we been on the road Nanny would have hustled us into a gateway while they passed.

I recall my embarrassment and disappointment when the cowman felt impressed to look up one day and saw me and proffered some teasing remarks about my perch. I did not like this practical jovial creature bursting into my secret world in this way, much as I liked him when we met him with Nanny down below.

I had a vivid imagination and in the security of the garden loved telling myself stories. I invented a whole series of imaginary people. My chief character was called 'My Lady'. The name was given more in a sense of denoting personal possession than social snobbery for her full name when I used it was just plain Mrs Dartchet. She had two children, a boy called Stanley and a girl whose name I can't recall. There was also an astonishing woman called Miss Hallicum who was, quite unblushingly, the mother of seven children. I could never make out why the grown-ups always smiled discreetly at each other when I mentioned that fact. I saw nothing wrong with it myself and as I was very serious about my imaginary friends I was very much put out by their apparent amusement over this matter.

I liked to walk alone round the kitchen garden when telling myself stories about these people. I often carried a little whip in my hand because I found it helpful to emphasise any surprising statement about their adventures by making gestures with it. When it was wet and I could not go out I used to sit on the old dappled grey rocking horse in the nursery and tell myself the same tales as I rocked to and fro rhythmically riding through miles of uncharted lanes in the immediate atmosphere.

At five years old I began to write and started my first novel, an historical one about the days of Roundheads and Cavaliers, a period of history that has always fascinated me. I still have the story. It is written in an old *Boots* scribbling diary of my mother's which she had discarded, because characteristically she had only had time to make one entry in it. My story opened with the dramatic lines:

'Stand villain or I draw my sword.'
It was Sir Rupert's angry voice that thundered through the gaunt old hall. The two men stood face to face.

The whole thing was so spontaneous. I only wish I found it as easy to write the first paragraph of a book in these more sophisticated days. I did not get very far with the story but even by then I had decided that I wished to be a writer. It seemed the natural thing for me.

There was always this inner world which I felt instinctively. I knew too that it had depths but depths that I could hardly prove in the conscious mind. 'We know and do not know,' as T.S. Eliot wrote in *Murder in the Cathedral.*'

It was when my brother and I were out in the kitchen garden at night that I knew instinctively a little more of this inner world. Darkness made these intuitive faculties more alert, like a wireless which will pick up distant stations far better in the dark. On warm summer nights we were allowed to go out on mothing expeditions. Although we did not kill promiscuously, we followed the mistaken habit of our generation of taking one of each species for our 'collection'. This habit I now deplore, as most people would, I think, because there were literally hundreds of little boys and girls who had 'collections' since it was the fashion to possess them and the destruction of moths was enormous.

The kitchen garden seemed full of these majestic creatures fluttering from flower and fruit bushes, brushing past one's face with velvet softness. When we netted some rare specimen whose image I had venerated for years in a coloured picture in the nursery moth book, my sense of wonder and awe was tremendous.

At night too the whole garden seemed alive with exciting scents which further alerted the senses. The tang of box hedges mingled with the fragrant smell of evening primroses and night scented stocks. These, the thrill of being up late and the coolness of the night air, all filled me with a feeling of exhilaration and expectation.

There was a strange old stone trough in the kitchen garden against the back wall of the coach house that bordered the garden on the west side. Far bigger than most troughs and with oddly rounded corners, it was full of stagnant water which gave off an odour of slime mingled with the scent of a white tea rose that flowered prolifically on the wall. I was very fond of standing by this at night and it was significant that one of the most vivid dreams of my life, which unlike most dreams I shall never forget, was pictured here.

Above the trough high up, was a round hole in the wall with a wooden shutter across it. This gave access to the loft and was intended to be used to stack hay through, I suppose.

One night I dreamt that I came into the garden and the shutter was open. There inside the loft, lying on a pile of hay, I saw a gigantic man dressed in some sort of armour with a huge winged helmet. I remember he was snoring violently and the sight of him filled me with an appalling horror. I crept by lest he should wake and see me. I remember being aware that his coming there had changed our whole lives and I said to myself, 'How dreadful, we can never again feel happy and safe and enjoy life as we did before.' It seemed that this man was a kind of permanent terror that had come upon us.

Later on when I came to read the history of the Vikings and their raids on the north west coast of England and to discover my great affinity with Norway, and with a particular place in the English Lakeland which had been a Viking settlement, I began to see that this dream might possibly have had some special significance for me if there is such a thing as remembering previous lives.

In spite of this dream I felt very attracted in my conscious life to this spot by the old trough and often stood at night, enveloped in soft summer darkness listening to the pip-pip of the colliery engines, and the mysterious whirr of the hedge stocks lowering the cage into the earth until they seemed like some giant vibrating into Eternity. And later on, lying in the cosy safety of the nursery, but still traversing in the mind's eye the outside world, I would hear the heavy rumble of distant goods trains lumbering through the night and felt the sensation of endlessly turning wheels rolling on whilst everywhere people lay wrapped in sleep, oblivious to what I felt and knew was the rhythm of space and eternity.

IV

In the Nursery with Nanny

The house that we loved so well would not have seemed a welcoming one to the casual passer-by, for it was of a rather severe style and fronted on to the north which was always sunless and cold. There was a wide gravel path up to the front door, which had neither the grandeur of the carriage drive at Hixon nor the intimacy of a garden path flanked with flowers. The entrance was through a thick archway one might almost call a tunnel of closely clipped thorn which provided a certain cosy niche in the bleak surroundings. There was an iron gate across it made of thin rails, but each was topped with a broad pointed end, a cross between an arrow head and a sceptre which must have been put there, I suppose, to give it some ecclesiastical dignity.

On each side of the front door, forming a foreground to the restricted windows of mock gothic were two formal flower beds, with a deep band of clipped ivy round them of the cold dark green variety, which never strayed off into the variegated trailers we knew on the ground and up tree trunks in the woods. It was very difficult to find anything that would grow there so these borders generally remained barren and empty. They are memorised by some photos, done by a local photographer, of my father standing in front of them in his clerical straw hat. I think I had wondered why they were taken there instead of against the more cosy setting of the shrubbery by the back yard where the rest of the family ones were done. One day, years afterwards, Nanny divulged that Daddy had been rather irritated when the local photographer, bidden perhaps by my mother who managed most domestic things, turned up and had refused to participate in this rather feminine occasion of the family group. Then, being a very kindly person really, he had regretted his impatience so had called the photographer back another day and had these taken on his own to propitiate, choosing the more severe manly setting of the front drive.

There always seemed to be a cold wind at the front door, what Nanny called 'a lazy wind', i.e. one that does not go round you. One could hear it moaning sometimes in a weird way when you were in the hall. The door itself was very plain with one severe pane of glass about the size of a large portrait frame that let a cold light into the hall, and in winter since it was not double-glazed in those days, the cold air. Its chief asset was that it enabled one to get a picture of the impending visitor before they were let in, if you crouched down in the privacy of the dark front staircase which went up at the side of the hall.

After they had rung the bell it was intriguing to see them standing there as if framed in a portrait, which suddenly came alive as they gave a nervous tweak to straighten their tie, or in the case of a lady adjusted a rather large and perilously perched hat, disturbed by the sharp north wind, before a domestic opened the door.

It generally seemed to be Nanny who did this, especially during afternoon calling hours, because she could be trusted to produce the silver salver ready for the cards if Mummy was out or open the sitting room door properly and show the lady in, not going first and then saying 'Yer can cum in' as some of our simpler domestics we had from time to time in the kitchen might have done. In those days there was a tremendous ritual about these things. The war had not commenced and my mother had not yet responded to her urge to drop the conventional and take action against it by giving up servants. In fact Nanny told me a most astounding story of how she had a very pretty blue pinafore given for Christmas and she asked my mother if she could wear it sometimes instead of her white apron. Even my unconventional mother had felt forced to reply:

'Well, Nanny, perhaps sometimes when we are quiet and alone, but never if there is anyone staying in the house or a "caller" likely to come to the front door.'

It was obvious that it caused her so much embarrassment

that Nanny never pursued the matter.

This story came to my knowledge many years later when Nanny, being crippled by a stroke, was unable to get out and buy her own clothes. When I suggested buying her a coloured cardigan she shook her head and begged for grey or black, saying that she had spent so much of her life in a uniform consisting of those colours that she never felt happy in anything else.

The entrance to a house in those days was a great class divider. Certain people went to the back door and others to the front according to their social status. For some reason the postman always came to the front, perhaps because he had the dual duty of delivering letters and collecting the outgoing ones from the silver salver on the hall table. One rather strange character availed himself of this privilege by using the hall as a kind of local sorting office, sitting cross-legged on the hearth rug and putting the mail into separate bundles all round him for the next houses he had to call at.

Then there was Bernard who evidently knew a good thing when he saw it. After having become a close friend of the family he expounded to my mother one day in his slow, rather dreary voice the story of a poor cripple who urgently needed a new pair of boots. My mother, who was well aware of the genuine poverty and want of such people, quickly procured a pair, only to see him wearing them himself a week later. When my mother expostulated about this he replied quite unperturbedly: 'Oh well, yer see Mum, I thought I would do myself a good turn for a change!'

Beside the fireplace in the sloping angle of the stairs was a fine oak cradle that had been in my father's family for years. My mother, brought up in the Victorian tradition of modesty was horrified when as a young bride a fat lusty woman from the parish saw it and remarked: 'Oh, I see you have brought your fruit basket with you.'

That was nothing to the remarks that the second groom from the Hall made to Nanny when he kindly brought the utility model purchased ready for my reception from the station in her Ladyship's dog cart. It was made of basket and was lined with oceans of frilly tulle, characteristic of the romance and mystery that surrounded a happy event in those days, which usually took place in the home.

That these articles of furniture should be the occasion for such jokes and blushes would seem ridiculous today when most people have acquired taciturn acceptance of such events and they are mostly regulated to the sparsely furnished hygienic sphere of the Labour Ward in hospital.

The rest of the hall furniture was old oak, except for one strange anomaly which seemed to be functionally indispensable in those days. This was the hat stand which stood at the back of the hall. It was made of faked old oak, ornamented by factory carving, on a back panel, and a mirror to check on one's appearance before going out, a matter of serious importance in those conventional days. Beside the mirror hung a clothes brush for an attentive maid to brush her employer's coat with should anything be found amiss. There were pegs at the back of considerable length to ensure that top hats could be safely hung on them.

On each side of the stand were rails set rather high and deep trays on tin below to accommodate the long umbrellas of those days and safely store the large quantities of rain that dripped from them.

The main room off the hall was the drawing room, a dark formal room, which my mother used to inveigh against as 'a nasty cold place'. It was only used on formal occasions when we had important visitors or Mummy's relatives came to stay, so it never got warmed by the family's presence.

The windows, framed in mock gothic style tracery, which let in little light, were softened by ninon curtains edged with Regency frills. Nanny was very clever at re-dipping these a soft saffron yellow every time they were washed, which brightened things up. The dye was made of an exciting potion of coffee and some other ingredient known only to her, and the effect was much admired.

This was, of course, only one of Nanny's special accomplishments brought out to help Mummy with her problems. That was what was so wonderful about her, that she was not one of those rigidly professional figures ruling the roost in her own nursery apartments, but she gave of her all to us unstintingly, participating in the family life wherever she was needed. It was, I suppose, because of this that she seemed a permanent part of it and although she had to leave us when I was not very old we never lost her as a devoted friend.

The carpet in the drawing room as I remember it seemed a large area of olive green for the room was sparsely furnished, alarming to cross when making any formal debut there. This colour hardly added to the warmth of the room. It was chiefly memorised in the family for the occasion when a local lady of title called and became caught up in denouncing the 'Lloyd George' as the new social insurance was then called. Striding up and down the green sward in, for her, a most unconventional way, she spoke with fury of this interference with her domestic arrangements and declaring that she would never stick on the stamps. She little knew that in a few years' time ladies would be pacing their drawing room floors in agitation because there were no servants left to stick the stamps on for.

Red baize doors were put up across the back of the hall, an attempt to divide the house into two classes, the gentry at the front and the servants at the back, the baize absorbing all kitchen sounds or cooking smells which might annoy. The back stairs, which were the ones nearest the nursery, came down behind these, which was convenient for us children as it gave us easy access to the kitchen. Ironically, the dining room, by some strange error of planning was entered by a door in the back hall not the front. For this reason it became the central family sitting room and in winter we scarcely entered the icy cold front part of the house shut off by the baize doors.

There was one historic occasion which Nanny used to recount when I burst through them like a whirlwind, letting them slam to behind me exclaiming, 'Oh, what a beast of a brother I've got.' As he was five years ahead of me I was always striving to imitate him and to catch up. He being a child of an age when teasing and practical jokes were the fashion, did not hesitate to take advantage of my admiration. Perhaps I felt better having broken through into the deserted part of the house where I could cool off.

The back stairs interested me very much because at night I used constantly to dream I was running down them so fast that my feet did not always touch the ground, and I was quite unable to stop till I reached the bend nearly at the bottom where the wall came directly across my path.

I learned later the interesting fact that some of Daddy's sisters dreamt this also, but Ralph had a recurring dream like my mother that he was falling from a great height. As I was said to resemble my father's family and Ralph my mother, this might point to the dreams being some inherited factor.

The kitchens were not bright, hygienic places like modern ones today. The floors were of an old-fashioned blue brick common to the north, which made them hard and chilly. The back kitchen was dominated as in the old days by a copper and a heavy mangle for there were no washing machines then. The front kitchen had an old-fashioned kitchener of black iron. It broke down in latter years during the war and being too old and costly to mend my mother cooked on oil and carried the bath water all the way upstairs.

But that was at a later date. When Nanny lived with us the old grate glowed with black lead polish and the touch of brass on the grate shone, it was a cosy place. The view from the window was, unfortunately, limited because in keeping with the current Victorian ethic that servants should be stowed away out of sight the high rockery and shrubs that guarded the entrance to the kitchen garden had been placed just opposite the window.

I do not recall Mrs Cash ever in this kitchen – the stout lady who collided with my mother in the doorway when Blériot's plane went overhead. Perhaps she was merely a temporary at Hixon Vicarage for I recall a strange story she told us of how she fell into the lock at the canal nearby when she was carrying a large basket of washing. Somehow her bulk and the washing basket kept her afloat in a wonderful way sufficiently long for a man to come along and pull her out!

On the whole I think all the occupants of our kitchen were young and of the type of Alice described in Nanny's letter because we could not afford the senior type of professional cook. Those that I can recall are mostly immortalised in my mind by their names, such as 'Little Ada' too small to be remembered, and 'New Dab'. The latter name I rather think was invented by us children. It probably originated from the fact that Nanny used to talk about 'dabbing things up' rather than wiping them. It meant a short, quick thrust at the foreign body to be removed rather than a wipe or wash over a large area. Perhaps New Dab was given to skimp her domestic duties which earned her this name.

Whatever she was like at housework she was certainly gifted on the piano, which caused us children to seek her entertainment in the sitting room at times. She played in a gay, fluent way that pleased us.

When my mother was expecting me as a baby, in order to save her too much work Granny paid the extra wages for us to have a pukka cook, Nanny's sister, Eleanor, for a whole year. She came to be known as 'Tippo'. The family album contains her photograph looking very smart and good-looking in a beautifully fitting uniform and curiously enough a very smart straw hat. It is of a rather severe sailor type which she seems to wear with a stylish air, and was quite in keeping with the uniform.

The reason she was called Tippo was because in those days the leading children's comic was *The Rainbow* about which my brother was extremely keen. Everyone had to take part in acting the stories and Eleanor took the part of Hippo, but somehow became altered to Tippo, perhaps by a childish slip of the tongue.

Nanny was wonderful at imitating Joey the parrot, though how she could transform her quiet, gentle voice to the raucous shrieks she gave out when acting the part I do not know. But she was such a star turn at it that she was constantly referred to by everyone, including my mother, as Joey for the rest of her life. My brother played the fierce male part of Tiger Tim, which he enjoyed very much.

Perhaps Nanny enjoyed putting over the fiercer side of her character in this fictitious role for of course she was not a dull, completely angelic creature with no likes and dislikes. She could get furious when people contravened the existing social stations though not, of course, having any logical awareness of why she did it.

A particular bête noire was when a school teacher married a clergyman. She was always very sniffy about the lady. I suppose this was because in her day the clergyman was very much the head of the village community, the father figure in a remote way. He was often the younger brother of the squire and therefore very definitely of the gentry and a university-educated man, which was rather more rare in those days among teachers in the village.

Then too, there was the clergyman's problem of choice. In those days when sex was thought to be something naughty and worldly goods an important criterion for eligibility in marriage, shy impecunious young curates were rather prey for the bossy type of woman without great feminine attractions, who made up their minds for them.

My mother had contact with this type at Mothers' Meetings, etc., and often felt there was a lot to be said for the Catholic idea of priests not marrying at all.

Of course, Nanny's criticisms did not stop at school teachers. She was quite unaware of what a delicious sociological definition she invented when she remarked one day by way of explanation of the behaviour of a self-made man whom she did not approve of:

'You see, dear, he is one of those jumped up knock you down sort of little men.'

Another of her dislikes were cats, not through any malicious dislike but because she was one of those people who were unable to touch them without some sort of revulsion. I think that some day this will be scientifically explained when we have studied people's electric fields further. I recall that the extremely disciplined courteous wife of the headmaster of Ralph's prep. school who had the same characteristic, a kind of built-in radar for detecting them. For when she came to tea and we thought that we had put every cat out of the room and shut the door firmly, she still declared that she could feel one in it. On a search being made she proved quite right. One had crept back under the sofa.

It was most unfortunate that Nanny disliked these animals because we loved them and had several of them all the time she was with us.

I well recall the first one which was given to me personally by our doctor's wife. I can still see Merrylegs drawing the governess cart into the yard, driven for some reason by Thornton, the retired coachman from the Hall, and recall my excitement when he got out carrying a square cardboard box, for I knew what was in it.

When I unpacked it there was a lovely grey persian kitten, with golden eyes looking at me. We called her Lady Grey. She lived with us till a ripe old age. I still have a photo of her, sitting elegant and placid in the sun, framed in the window of our new Vicarage to which she moved with us years later.

Whether the news got around with the arrival of this lovely grey creature that the Vicarage was a good place for cats I do not know, but I recall that the week Lady Grey arrived we acquired five cats altogether, counting little Blackie who was already resident, the last one having been surreptitiously introduced into my father's vestry during evensong.

My mother added to the collection at a later stage by bringing back a kitten from her own home, which had been born in a rabbit hole. Perhaps it was this early contact with what we now call a feral cat that did something to involve me in their present problems and develop my concern to see this form of cruelty eliminated.

'Ma', as the kitten was called, grew up a delightful but rather pathetic figure. A clearly marked tabby, she never gained the comfortable plumpness of the other cats. We never discovered why – perhaps because she seldom rested and was nearly always sitting lean and upright, looking apprehensively into the distance, as if she was worried about what would appear. In those days we called it 'Looking for Germans'. Perhaps it was the anxiety her mother had felt when having kittens to guard in a wild state, but in spite of this apprehension of distant danger she was tremendously affectionate to those near to her and so grateful for any kindness and understanding.

Our cats were quite famous locally for my brother became a good amateur photographer at quite a young age. He entered one for a competition in the local paper *The Staffordshire Sentinel*. He hit on the idea of getting the cats to gather round a huge dish of milk, with Lofty, a docile, timid hound sitting beside them. She was inwardly very much in awe of the cats, who sometimes made quite unprovoked attacks on her when they had kittens. So she sat there, very still and worried looking, not daring to turn her head. As it was March he titled it appropriately 'Her Lenten Fast'. It won first prize, which caused great family excitement.

Nanny had three sisters and they were all in service. Clara, the eldest one, was lady's maid to a parson's daughter of some affluence in Hampshire. She was a very precise, tidy person, who was wonderful at making scrap books of those cards which they had in those days, reflecting the Victorian sentiment of family life.

She once came to see us at Hixon but there was an event terribly near disaster. I don't recall her crossing our threshold ever again.

Ralph had a bow and arrow, a somewhat fashionable toy of those days, unfortunately. He showed it to Clara on the lawn, demonstrating his prowess by shooting an arrow at some considerable length. I insisted on being allowed to try to give a demonstration too. My brother laughed at this idea contemptuously, proceeding to fix me up with an arrow for a shot, assuring Clara that I could never do it as I always dropped the thing. Unfortunately, Clara did not take into account that most of this was brotherly sarcasm. For once I did do it and the arrow shot into the air towards Clara who was standing right in front of me, hit her cheek and sailed on into the bushes. Blood spurted forth from the gash and poor Clara beat a hasty retreat into the house to receive comfort from Nanny. I don't recall ever seeing her again.

Edith, known as Edie, Nanny's younger sister, completed the family's qualifications in domestic duties by becoming a parlour maid. For a short time she went to my grandmother (on my mother's side) and was known as the only parlour maid who was not frightened of my fierce old hunting grandfather. He liked her very much because of this and was heard to remark, 'That woman's got brains!'

Unfortunately, she left after a short time, like most of Granny's maids. She went to my father's sister, Auntie Bea, who had just married a rather grumpy widower. He was actually her sister Evie's father-in-law, so by this marriage she became mother-in-law to her own sister. He was not as actively fierce as my grandfather and Edie really got great amusement in dodging some of his disciplinary regulations with which he ruled the household and helping Auntie Bea, who made a close friend of her, in many crises.

I always regarded Auntie Bea with special interest as I was

at one time said to be like her. 'She is rather like her Auntie Bea' relatives used to say reflectively, or 'Put's me in mind of Miss Bea,' the people in the parish repeated. She had 'kept house' in a very vague way for my father for a time before he married. As time went on my hair got less auburn than hers and the commentary ceased. Only Nanny kept up the link because when I was slow owing to preoccupation with my imaginary world she used to say, 'You are getting so dawdling, dear, you put me in mind of Miss Bea.'

Auntie Bea seemed to be a rather mixed up sort of person for her sisters spoke of her as having been the tomboy of the family when young, but she was the very opposite of this when we knew her in later life. She was a typical Edwardian figure with eyeglasses and large hats. She wore capes and used a black ebony stick to support herself when walking but when talking to you she would sink down into the nearest chair, with an exhausted sigh, rather like a Jane Austen character, and tell you all about the latest doctor she had visited. She made rather a habit of seeing them.

In her later years she developed a great taste for cosiness so she used to winter in the South of France, till she became so dependent on the sunshine and warmth she settled there permanently. When war came and most of her contemporaries with British passports fled home, she did not make the slightest effort to move. She simply stayed on at the same pension as if nothing had happened.

Not even an advancing army of German Nazis and the possibility of their engaging in war there could disturb her. She was very wise really for she was far too old to be a political liability. The Germans just left her there like a cat curled up in the sun. She lived through the war all right but died quite soon after it before any of the family could get out to see her, for which we were very sorry.

During her married life she lived at a big house near Hixon, just beyond the level crossing. She was rather fond of society, and curiously enough she had my liking for trimming hats. On one occasion she imparted to Edie how pleased she was as she heard there was to be a fête in the village.

'I can just do with a little gaiety like that,' she said, 'but I must have a nice hat for it.'

Economy did not allow her to buy a new one so she got some hat dye and painted an old one a lovely blue, and then piled flowers on it as was the custom then. She set out in great delight to display it at the fête. But, unfortunately, it came on to rain terrifically, as it does in the north, the dye was not rainproof. Suddenly blue streaks came streaming down her face and she had to rush home in great haste to avoid terrible social embarrassment, much to the amusement of Edie who helped to wash it off.

V

A Cold Front

The dining room was a lovely room, large enough to serve both as sitting room and a room to feed in but it never seemed vast and unfriendly. It was situated under the nursery and had the same sunny facing looking on to the lawn with the wistaria climbing round the window.

My father had a wonderful court cupboard with small doors inlaid with tulip wood in rather a rococo style, which had come from my great grandfather's house in Cheshire. Beside this stood a vast gateleg table of oak at which my father and his ten brothers and sisters had all had lessons in their country vicarage nursery near Stafford, where my grandfather was vicar for fifty years.

Now it was the centre of entertaining of all kinds from high teas for parishioners to the more formal occasions. When a visiting clergyman came to preach and partook of cold supper after the evening service Nanny would be called upon to do what was known as 'Nanny's Sweet'. This was a special blancmange of a subtle pale yellow colour, being made, I think, considerably of real eggs. It was very light and floating, almost like a soufflé. Made in an old-fashioned copper mould which was called a honeycomb, it looked like a picture from Mrs Beaton when turned out and placed in the centre of the table.

My mother would always thank Nanny warmly on these special occasions saying, 'Well done', but Nanny, essentially modest and respectful before an employer, even one who was a personal friend, would only blush and cast her eyes down and murmur in her soft voice:

'It's all right, Madam.'

It was a valuable contribution to the meal, which had to be

taken without the help of my father to entertain the guest since they would generally exchange pulpits. It brought a more individual character to the food and broke the traditional idea created by a bishop who said that visiting parish churches for evening service meant to him perpetual cold roast chicken and 'Nearer my God to Thee'.

Nanny took great pride in helping to deck the table for special events. My parents were lucky in having some lovely wedding presents given them but these really made a façade of riches beyond their means and were sometimes an embarrassment. There was the occasion when I was very ill and an infant specialist was sent for from Birmingham to see me. Nanny laid out a most lovely tea for him with a Crown Derby tea set we had and some nice bits of silver. He enjoyed this very much but when the bill came it was terrific. Presumably, he thought by this rather scrumptious tea table that we were well off and could pay it.

This illness was, I believe, quite a dramatic episode in our nursery and family life. The trouble started when my mother had no milk and was unable to feed me so I had to be put on a bottle. I developed thrush and the doctor complained to the monthly nurse about lack of cleanliness over the bottle teats which he thought had probably caused this. This led her to give me excessive doses of boracic to clear the trouble up which set up boracic poisoning. I became desperately ill and I had thirty-two convulsions one night, or so family history goes, but I have always wondered, knowing the consternation they must have caused, how anyone managed to count them! It was thought that night that I would be unlikely to recover but in some extraordinary way I did.

My illness led to another innovation in the household, a wet nurse. The one found was the rather hearty wife of a local butcher's assistant. He used to come and see his wife regularly on a bicycle which bore a large placard hung from the cross-bar 'Fresh Meat Daily'. She had, of course, to move into one of the nurseries with her sturdy little son, for whom she also had plenty of milk, I am glad to say. Her reliance on the butcher's shop seems to have extended to many spheres, for when making her bed Nanny was disturbed to find a well-chewed chicken bone which she gave to her baby instead of a dummy.

Luckily, though surprisingly, there was no vicarage tragedy through him swallowing it. A recent book on this subject points out that it was a prevalent belief that the baby drew certain characteristics from the wet nurse in the mother's milk. I certainly did not acquire any love of meat from her, having been a vegetarian since my thirties. I suppose I am rather direct and energetic, a characteristic accounted for partly because I am a Sagittarian. It may well be that I received some of the robustness of the butcher's wife for she was only chosen after extensive enquiries into her family history and she was said to be very strong and healthy.

It is tremendously to Nanny's credit that this sudden innovation of another nurse into her domain, not a meek little underling but a mature woman of independent personality never seems to have caused any friction, nor did it prevent her having as great an affection for me as for my brother Ralph in spite of the fact that she had heralded my advent with alarm. She watched over me with the same care and interest in my development in every detail as the following letter which my mother kept shows.

Dear Mistress,

2.15. We are not out quite so early today as I stayed to do the wash ready. Babs did so enjoy counting out the things. I have got the basket down all ready. I thought Edith would not have to come up at night for it if Babs was asleep. Managed laddie's bath very nice last night, Babs did not wake. She is such a lot better in her inside since you left out the cream, not at all curdled now. She has gone in her pram today without a murmur. I'm so glad as I think she seemed a bit tired this morning. Bobbin has got the puppies playing with him. He is being very good on the whole today, he had such a naughty teasing fit while I was cutting the dinner, had to send him into the dining room until all was quite ready – it did him good for he was so good over his dinner, ate so nicely. He is not good over tea when Edith is with us though, quite different to being by himself he is all the time, trying to make her laugh.

I see today his grey coat is all in a rag at the bottom of the sleeves. I have put him in it today as the wind is much colder it is North East. Only one more day before you return now I wonder if you have seen the babies.

Mrs Coclough (I don't know if I've spelt it right) came the other day to see about her baby been christened. She said she'd heard you had a pram to sell and she wanted one. She said how much did you want for it. I thought perhaps she wouldn't be able to pay for it and you wouldn't like to keep asking her for the money when she hadn't got it so I said yes, I did know because there was a person coming to look at it and you'd told me what you wanted for it and not to let her take it unless I had the money as you couldn't afford to give it away, so last night she came down with a dish the Master had bought of her Mother. She told me to tell you if you had not sold your pram if you'd keep it until June her husband would have sent her some money then and she could have it then as you didn't want it to go without the money.

The Master has brought Bobbin, (his pet name for my brother), and Babs a pink and white china house each, Babs is very fond of hers.

Bobbin's message, 'tell her I could do with that record, 'French bonnet' on one side and 'Kelly' on tother, you can give me love to her'. Baby's message, booful day baby Angel, Babba in booful air.

I suppose you will send order for Beeftea meat for Saturday.

Yours very respectfully,
Nan

Perhaps this acceptance of the wet nurse was helped by the close friendship between Nanny and my mother so that she never felt she was being put on and they could laugh together, discreetly about the chicken bone in the baby's bed, which became a sort of family joke that was handed down to us. Of course, the wet nurse's stay was only temporary and when I was old enough to have a bottle Nanny got her nursery back and things went back to normal.

As I was four years younger than my brother, I was put to bed sometime before he was. Ralph, clad in blue cord-edged dressing gown, would sit on the righthand side of the fire,

Myself as a baby in Nanny's arms with my brother Ralph

Aged twelve

reading *The Gem* or *The Boy's Own Paper*. Nanny sat on the other side of the fireplace, plying her needle at some exquisite piece of sewing. She was an artist at such things, especially at smocking, mostly in pastel shades on white viyella frocks for me.

Our only means of lighting was by an oil lamp, and this stood on a table by the fireside, shaded from me by an old book cover with a picture of a boy and girl on it. An economy, I suppose, since in those days you could go out and buy a lamp-shade cheaply at a nearby chainstore. I am sure if anyone had commiserated with us in this make-do, however, we should have been most surprised. This cover was to us as much an individual object belonging to the room as some family portrait. I still have it put by in a drawer.

I would lie awake for a long time in the old-fashioned light oak bed, watching the scene drowsily in the cosy light. Now and then the coal would slip, and the flames would leap up in the grate, throwing strange patterns of shadow on the ceiling. Sometimes my brother would chuckle loudly at some adventure of the Fat Boy, Billy Bunter, to be admonished by Nanny in her soft voice, for fear he disturbed me.

Then, near Christmas, Nanny would set aside the routine sewing, and start on mysterious sewing activities, at which we were not supposed to look. I still recall a doll called Ivy, one of the many which Nanny dressed herself for me at Christmas, clad in a white Viyella frock, trimmed with lace and pink ribbons, and a cape of green velour – made from a piece left over from my winter coat. How well I remember seeing Nanny working on it, and a thrill of anticipation still seems to surround Ivy when I think of her.

Many things heightened the tempo of nursery life as Christmas drew nearer. There were the joys of the Christmas catalogues, with their gaudy pictures of toys and recently published books. I used to peer at the reproductions of each book plate with the intensity of a crystal gazer, wondering what the cover held, and whether this or that one would be seen on the nursery table in the near future.

Sometimes we caught a quick glimpse of something in Mummy's or Nanny's hand. On one occasion, it was a certain publication entitled *Princess Mary's Gift Book*. My brother confided to me his discovery, and how we enjoyed whispering

about it, and winking when my mother or Nanny were near –
just to show we knew something we ought not to.

Later, when this long anticipated volume became ours, we
did not understand a great deal of it really, as it was a grown-
up's publication, but that made it all the more exciting. I was
especially intrigued by the way the pictures were put in,
placed on a mount of discreet beige, and gummed only at the
top so that you could lift them up with your fingers and peep
underneath. Some of the poetry items I learnt by heart, for
example Kipling's 'Oh where are you going to, all you big
steamers?' Being always an enthusiast for the sea, I boomed
out the words with delight, but there was an ominous line I
avoided, which ran:

'And if anyone hinders our coming, you'll starve.'

Some days before Christmas, the smaller of the two
nurseries was shut up entirely, and only Nanny allowed to
enter it because of the dressing of the Christmas tree that was
placed in there. Decorations were not so prolific in the shops
in those days. Nanny kept the precious ornaments from year
to year, in a little rush basket that was fastened by a
fascinating peg handle. On the tree I chiefly remember
shining witch-balls and deliciously sticky pink sugar pigs and,
of course, *real* red and blue candles in tiny tin candlesticks,
that kept on tipping up on the tree and spilling grease about.

I recall one occasion when Nanny slipped away into the
little nursery. My brother rushed me to the window to see
Father Christmas jump out of the one next door. Ralph told
me that Father Christmas was at work on the tree and he
would be sure to be frightened away when Nanny went in.
Needless to say, I never saw him, so I suspected my brother's
story very much; in fact I think it shattered my belief in Father
Christmas entirely. Most of the information that Ralph gave
me was fictitious and given only to tease, I realised. I don't
think the Father Christmas myth was ever very important to
us, however. We got plenty of excitement, and satisfaction
from the family preparations, which seemed more natural and
real because to my mother and Nanny this festival meant so
much.

Then, when Christmas Eve came, and the preparations
were all done, the great moment would arrive when the cosy

evening peace by the nursery fire would be broken. Admonishments about going to sleep would be stilled. Then Nanny would open the window and let in the sound of the Christmas bells, pealing forth through the bitter air from the ancient octagonal tower of the church which we knew so well. How jubilant and happy they sounded! I did not realise then that in future years this sound would form a kind of mental ladder, down which would slide helter-skelter a hundred vivid memories of the past whenever I heard them again, and in so many places far away from my childhood home.

I have come to feel that the realities of these memories, which seem so clear to us still, will one day live again, in fact they do live on indefinitely, if we nurture them by awareness and love. It is like the reality of a friendship which exists, even though we may not meet the friend for years, and is there for us to gather up again when we meet, as if there had been no break. I believe, in the light of the knowledge I have gained, that when we reach the After Life, these 'memories' will be there on the mental plane, for us to enjoy once more, but in even greater happiness, united for ever with those loved ones who shared them with us on earth.

Music is a wonderful key for unlocking memories and another close link with my life then are certain familiar hymns. Hymn singing was part of our life. On the far side of the fireplace was a small upright piano, with brass candlesticks on brackets fixed to the sides. My mother played and sang very nicely. It was a pity that both before and after her marriage she was always too busy ministering to the needs of others to find time to develop her gift fully. On Sunday nights, however, she always spared time and we used to stand round the piano singing hymns whilst my mother played for us. Only those who have been brought up in this tradition can realise the indelible impression this makes on a child's mind.

The extraordinary thing was the diversity of moods and feelings they created, not linked objectively with the actual lines, but absorbed from a blending of the words and tune. These combined seemed to create a special atmosphere.

Some hymns seemed very depressing, not due to any grimness or preoccupation with hell fire (my parents were not strict Evangelicals or revivalists) but more to the feeling of

Victorian sentimentality that pervaded them. They were so cosily depressing, which made them the more unbearable. Often it was the hymns which helped the grown-ups most which had the worst effect on me. My mother, for instance, was very fond of the hymn:

> Oh, strength and stay upholding all creation!
> Who ever does Thyself unmoved abide.

On analysing the words as an adult, I realise that they are most reassuring, but to me, coupled with the sad, gentle melody that they were set to, they seemed to symbolise a beautiful but sodden Autumn evening, when everything was slowly disintegrating before our eyes. And when the lines continued:

> The brightness of a holy deathbed blending
> With dawning glories of the Eternal Day.

I felt no joy in that heavenly calendar, the mention of a *holy* deathbed filled me with just as much overwhelming fear as an ordinary one, and kept me from following the idea further into the glories that followed.

If only we had been given a more realistic attitude to the After Life as children, with their natural spontaneity and awareness of the unseen, we could have grasped it so readily. But the mantle of Victorian morbidity overlaid things still, and Barrie had only just made Peter Pan utter the then surprising sentiment 'To die would be an awfully big adventure.'

There were moments of spiritual elation, however, in these moving tunes, which seemed to imprint the mind with a permanent picture like a photograph, revelations to be stored away in one's collection of memories.

I shall never forget, for instance, the first confirmation I attended at the age of five, and singing the hymn 'Soldiers of Christ, Arise'. The throb of the organ, and the uplifting sensation of complete dedication thrilled me in a way I have never forgotten. No other confirmation, least of all my own, which took place at the self-conscious age of sixteen amongst a bevy of school girls determined not to do anything 'sloppy', ever came up to this first one. It has made me realise that there is much to be said for the Catholic custom of confirming a child early, before the crust of convention and a wish to do the correct thing has become a barrier to their instinctive perception of the spiritual.

And there were moments of jubilation, too, which remain in my mind. The great upsurge of voices as a group of united voices of the choir pealed forth the lines:

The valleys stand so thick with corn
That even they are singing!

What a landscape it evoked in the mind's eye! Sunshine and vast acres of glowing corn, spreading on the sloping sides of some great, open vale, and gently waving in the wind.

But the hymn that triumphed over all in its feeling of cosy and glorious security was the one which ran:

In token that thou shalt not fear,
Christ crucified for thee.

It was not so much the words, the full significance of which I never really understood, as the atmosphere and rhythm. We seldom sang it in church, as it was used mostly for christenings, but once heard it was never forgotten, and became a favourite request item from Nanny when she sang me to sleep in the nursery. How bravely her voice seemed to thrill upwards as she sang it! It was just the thing for rounding off the cosy security of the nursery on a winter night, and making it complete.

On looking back, I realise how tremendously that security mattered to me, and how much I feared the least breach in its defences. There were certain songs Nanny was not allowed to sing at all because they brought such an overwhelming feeling of sadness, which I knew deep down inside was really in the world, but I was determined not to recognise. I little knew how inevitably it would break in on us very soon.

VI

The War Clouds Break

The summer of 1914 found us back at Hixon again. Holidays there had become quite a habit. It was near my father's and mother's homes, and there were many old friends and relatives around for them to visit.

I do not recall events of much importance occurring at first. A visiting parson came to stay, who was so sporting as to let us tie him up in the study antimacassar, and play Blind Man's Buff. My brother learnt to ride his first bicycle under the tuition of the local policeman called P.C. Kettle, who held up the traffic for him, and he also learnt how to reach the anti-burglar hooks at the top of the doors into the hall. After this, he developed a horrible habit of locking me in the rooms, which produced a kind of claustrophobia and a fear that a lock won't undo which I have had ever since. But Nanny was always at hand to unlock the door and set me free from my terror.

Having exhausted this form of torture, however, Ralph produced another more subtle one, of a psychological kind. Suddenly he announced, with great firmness and importance: 'The Germans are coming here, and they will kill you!'

In one sentence he swept away the whole foundation of my world. Our entire security was threatened if this was so. I don't think I worried about my own personal safety, nor even that of my parents, for I thought we might escape from them in some way. But what frightened me terribly was that the Germans would kill my beloved cats, or if they were not killed, they would be frightened by the German invasion and would run away.

Sobbing, I ran to Nanny, expecting to have the fears my brother had set up in my mind dispelled as usual. She would be sure to say he was only teasing, telling me a fairy story, and she would make life normal and secure again.

But for the first time in my life, Nanny could not tell me that what Ralph said was untrue. She only hung her head! The Germans were going to attack us then? It seemed unbelievable. I went cold with fear.

A little later, when my mother entered the room I felt our fate was sealed. As far as I can recall Nanny was sitting downstairs with us, doing some mending, in the very rocking chair from which we had so joyously taken the antimacassar to play Blind Man's Buff with the parson.

'Nanny,' my mother said gravely, as if she knew what we were already talking of, 'Mr Ernest says that he is afraid there is going to be a war.'

Mr Ernest! My heart sank. It was a case of 'the importance of being Ernest'. He was the family oracle on all worldly affairs. He was my mother's only brother, and a lawyer who belonged to that strange business world where 'they' always knew what was going to happen and what to do about money and things like that. It was a world which my friendly, easy-going father seemed to have no part in, so we relied on Uncle Ernest entirely in this respect. His ideas depressed me with their inevitable logic, but his pronouncements were usually correct. Therefore, what Ralph said *must* be true!

I don't recall whether it was actually on August 4th that this conversation took place. I think it was probably a few days beforehand. But I remember the night of August 4th as clearly as if it was yesterday. I don't recall when, or where, I was told that the dreadful thing had come to pass, and war was actually declared. I only know that I was aware it had been, and I was convinced that the Germans might arrive at any moment. For me there was only one world, and it was formed by my immediate surroundings. Therefore, if the Germans were coming to fight us, they must come to Hixon. It never entered my head that hundreds of miles, and much water, separated us from them, and in those days, when armies had to march on foot, it would have taken weeks for a huge army to reach us. If only the grown-ups had explained things to me! They were generally so careful about my feelings, but perhaps I hugged my fears to myself, or they were too caught up in the international situation to notice.

All night long I lay in terror of what would come. I cannot remember any details of that nursery at Hixon, only that as I lay in bed I could see through the open door the top of the staircase and knew that there was a bend a few stairs down. It was round this bend, I was sure, that the Germans would come. I peopled the place with them so vividly in my mind's eye that, even now, I can see them as if they had really been there – tramping heavily up the stairs, enormous, heavy-breathing men in steel helmets, with that peculiar piece of curved metal over the top which symbolised for us all German soldiers then.

I must have fallen asleep at last from sheer nervous exhaustion, for suddenly I knew it was morning. I heard the click of the front gate. I lay terrified – certain now that they had really arrived, and were pushing it open. Actually, it was only the milkman. The steel latch on the gate made this sound every morning when he called: but roused suddenly from sleep with the idea of the Germans uppermost in my mind, I transformed even this familiar sound into an omen of danger. I cowered down under the bed clothes like a frightened animal – the fact that Nanny lay sleeping beside me made not the slightest difference. I must have had a realistic idea of war. I knew that Nanny, with all her protective love, could be no use against an army of soldiers.

For a long time I lay there shaking, and then, as nothing happened, the tension slowly loosened. I felt vague and empty. Nanny got up, and someone referred to the milkman's morning call. My terror fell away in the light of day and the morning's bustle as a normal day began again.

At first sight, it would appear a pity that I experienced this terror, which could have been dispelled had the grown-ups understood the situation. But I have come to feel that this was no chance happening in my life, in fact I think that few major happenings are. Of course, I did not know then that many years later my work was to be among European nationals who had actually fled from such invading armies, or lived under the threat of the Gestapo. That is something we can hardly imagine when we have lived in a country as free as ours has been for so many centuries. It is difficult to appreciate the terror of life when, at any moment, in the dark hours of the night, there might come a battering on the door, and we should be forced to open it and see a member of the family led away to torture and death.

At least I could share something of the reality of this with those who had suffered, by recalling that night of August 4th which has always remained so vividly in my mind.

I suppose when the Germans did not come, the acute fear wore off and we settled down to the normal routine of life. My father was too old to join up as a chaplain. For his war work he took on visiting in a parish in the Potteries, where they were short of curates. He also became a special constable, wearing a striped armlet and carrying a truncheon, which caused much amusement in the family, not sorrow and parting as many had to face in those days.

Returning to our permanent home again broke the link with memories of the terrors of the night of August 4th. We were so lucky in having few close relatives involved in it. Two older cousins were killed in France whom I had never met. Only occasionally in isolated episodes did the tragedy of war cross our path through happenings to our friends, which made it seem a more personal event.

During the winter I was inaugurated into a strange social event, the dancing class. There were not many parties we could attend in those days owing to the difficulties of travelling home in an open governess cart on a winter night, so a very popular event among parents, giving an opportunity for social contacts, both adult and juvenile, was the dancing class which took place in the early afternoon. I never enjoyed this myself; I found it a very alarming experience to be placed in the middle of a large unfurnished area of brown wood and expected to perform – often solo – while admiring and critical parents sat round the room staring at us. It was the first time I had ever been called on to 'appear in public' and as if one's footsteps in life were not complicated enough, I found in this dancing world that there were dogmatic positions arranged for the feet to fit into with each blaring number on the piano.

They were apparently concrete facts universally understood by everyone else like the squares on some gigantic pediatric chess board but to me, with my inaptitude for arithmetic, it was a lost world. I was always the last to get my feet into the correct shape when the terrifying order was given – 'Now children, take your position please, bend the knees ready.' The twanging piano would start off, the pianist thumping out the exercise, the music gathering momentum like a runaway car on a hill. I knew for myself at any rate it was only a matter of time before we ended in a crash.

I only remember two of these positions now. The first, to let you down easily I suppose, consisted of putting one's heels together with the feet slightly turned out. The fifth was a terror and calculated to sum up all the inexplicable knots you were to tie yourself into as the class progressed. It consisted of putting the heel of one foot and the toe of the other together so that one's feet were completely disabled for any forward or backward progress. Having entered into this trap you were expected, with the aid of a chair to steady you, to go up and down like a concertina, bending your knees rhythmically.

After you had persevered for some time at these 'five finger' or rather five toe exercises, one was promoted to more mobile forms of activities with strange sounding French names such as *pliés*, etc. The only one that really appealed to me, however, was the *bronjéte*, because in this you hurl yourself up into the air recklessly, bringing the legs together and swinging round in mid air. It had something of the elation of flying upward for a brief space before you descended abruptly to reality. How often I wished I could stay up there instead of coming down to the disturbing medley below.

Bronjétes were followed by more complicated and pictorial forms of activity, dances which went by specific names and in which we were all expected to join. There was one which I specially remember which went by the picturesque title of 'Fairy Tip Toes'. It was inaptly named, since it was anything but tiptoes we employed for its execution. Perhaps the early part was faintly reminiscent of the name, but it was not sufficiently dramatic to remain in my memory. As the dance progressed it gained a terrific momentum and one was forced to leave the sheltered 'nursery slopes' where we had stood in orderly lines and career forward, bending and jumping upward alternately like a rearing horse, while we lifted each foot high enough to touch the opposite knee. 'Higher, children, higher,' would come a frantic cry from near the piano as we plunged forward, led by the local accountant's daughter, who, being much taller than most of us and very conscientious, always seemed to be first in the race. Unfortunately, as her conscientiousness increased she compensated for the mental strain by putting out her tongue and twisting it to the side of her mouth in a most peculiar way. The grotesqueness of this gesture, coupled with the thundering stampede, quite eliminated any atmosphere of the romantic fairy queen, as I presume a successful rendering of the dance was intended to do.

The dancing class was, I suppose, a necessary point of social contact, even though it was not a very successful one. In those days mothers set great store by the accomplishments we learnt there in general grace and social decor, and it gave them a chance to meet together and chat.

My brother came to the class too until he went to boarding school and developed a special attachment for a girl called Mildred which lasted throughout his life.

Part of its value was the opportunity we children had of meeting other children. How carefully and almost suspiciously we inspected one another and our appearances when we met. This added a great interest in the advent of any newcomer in the class. On the whole they were quite a nice group and we made, I think, some good friends from it.

There was one girl who wore a glorious green silk dress which I very much admired. She was dark and it suited her exceedingly. I don't recall what I wore myself – probably one of Nanny's smocks in viyella, to keep me warm, as this was such a concern of my mother and although it had exquisite handiwork on it, it had not the glamour of some dresses like the green silk to attract the other girls' eyes.

One day, however, when we came to the class the girl's mother was in tears and mine, being a sympathetic person, sought to find out the reason. Apparently, the lady's husband had been killed in the war recently and the very same week she had discovered that the family business, carried on incompetently in his absence, had gone bankrupt. She had been forced to dismiss all her servants immediately, including the groom. She had no idea how to harness the pony herself and seemed to have got things into an awful muddle and was worried about driving it home. My mother, luckily having had to lead a more practical life on a clergyman's meagre stipend, knew how to do it. She went out into the yard and soon helped to put the matter right. Later we were glad to hear that relatives had rallied round the family and they went to live in another town where there was a famous day school where children could be well educated at minimum cost.

One of the compensations of the dancing class for me was wearing bronze dancing shoes. They were carried in a discreet olive green string bag with white rings. Oh what joy when they were pulled out. My pleasure in them was somewhat inexplicable and has made me sympathetic towards the theories of colour healing and effects of that kind put forward by Rudolph Steiner and others though I have never had time to study these in detail. Oh, how those shoes seemed to vibrate in some way and fill me with delight. That cosy glow they gave off, so symbolic of glamour and the party, though I seldom went to parties in them.

During the winter Granny fell ill and my mother made several visits to her over at Chartley. A local journey in those days was quite an undertaking without any car, especially with snow on the ground. She had to walk two miles to the station as it was too slippery to take the pony out even though Merrylegs' shoes were 'roughed' for the winter.

On one particular journey she lost her most treasured brooch, a double cameo of onyx – two blue heads on a black border set in a circle of pearls. These had really been a pair of ear-rings of my great grandmother's and Granny had had them mounted together on one pin as a gift for Mummy. My mother and father felt too poor to offer a comparable reward for such a valuable brooch so they accepted the loss and did nothing about trying to find it which seemed rather strange – but in spite of this a chain of events brought it back to us.

Our life carried on much the same as usual with Nanny in charge, during my mother's visits away, but my mother, though trying to solve Granny's many problems, evidently still had us in mind. On one of her later visits when the cold spell became intense she became worried about our catching colds at the class. The 'Institution' where we took our classes was a rather dilapidated wooden hut of some considerable size next door to the church in a nearby parish where the railway station was situated. The walls were unlined and it was extremely cold in winter. My mother wrote to my father asking him to go and see the caretaker about making a fire there. The only form of heating it had was an old black stove with a pipe that went into the ceiling, a monstrosity of ugliness that appeared to have little effect on the heat of the room.

My father sought out the caretaker in a rather poor part of that parish, a place he never went to normally. She came to the door in a loosely fitting black blouse and, much to his surprise, he saw the neck was held together by an old cameo brooch. It was apparently the facsimile of the one that my mother had lost some months before. I remember how he came back and asked Nanny for details of it. She confirmed his idea that it was the right one by her description of it.

When my father spoke to the caretaker about it she said that her son had picked it up in the snow one morning after a baker's cart had gone over it, but it showed no damage. It was undoubtedly the missing brooch and so my father gave the woman a modest reward with which she seemed very satisfied and brought it back home.

Nanny put it away safely in a match box. Then a few days later we drove to the station with her to meet Mummy on her return home. I can still remember how when we were settled nicely in the pony cart and were on our way back Nanny placed the box on my mother's knee and said: 'There's a present for you, Madam.' My mother smiled appreciatively and then proceeded to open it in anticipation of some nice little trinket we had bought to amuse her. We sat on the other side of the cart watching her intently. I remember her delight when she lifted the lid and gave a cry of joy and surprise:

'Oh, Nanny, how wonderful.' There was the brooch of which she had been so fond, lying safely in the box! Certainly that brooch has been lucky for it has been lost again since then and found, but that is another story.

When summer approached we did not return to Hixon, I am not sure why. Perhaps because we did not want to be reminded of that first night of the War. When I discussed with Nanny many years after my traumatic experience at Hixon

Vicarage that night of August 4th, she told me she attributed it all to my mother's sister Aunt Nellie. Nanny had, apparently, accompanied us on an afternoon visit to see Granny at Chartley earlier in the week. Aunt Nellie had come in at tea time, full of the possibility of imminent war. She had suggested that we would come near starvation so we should therefore as families start buying food at once in large quantities. It was rather typical of her egotistical nature that she did not appear to think of the other families we would be depriving of food. She had always been the more dominant of the two sisters, who shone like a cold, glistening diamond in the family and in the county society she moved in. So over-looked was my mother that there is a story of how Granny, sitting ruminating over the breakfast coffee pot with my grandfather one morning, remarked:

'That young clergyman, George Plant, is coming here such a lot, I rather think he has fallen in love with Alice.'

Grandpa, without lowering *The Times*, merely replied: 'You mean Nellie.'

It seemed incredible that modest little Alice should have an admirer when the brilliant Nellie was around.

Perhaps this outburst of Aunt Nellie's on war produced a cheque from Granny for our next holiday in order that we should avoid going to that house of now unhappy memories. In some extraordinary way the money was forthcoming for a real holiday as paying guests, including Nanny. It was by this miracle that I was enabled to discover Wales, which being near the Midlands was to be our happy hunting ground for holidays for many years to come. My father adored Wales; it was to him something like Norway became to me. He had been there since his early youth. My grandfather owned a farm at Rhonfelin close to Plynlimon, where the Severn finds its source. I have never been able to discover why a clergyman who was fifty years vicar of a Midlands parish came by this, but he did and it was much appreciated.

The holiday at the farm was not a success for me. When I passed through that district recently and heard the thunder rumbling round the hills and the sheets of black clouds scurried across the sky and how heavy was the rain that poured down at regular intervals, I realised it was not the place for a nervous child. Only a grown-up could appreciate the landslip's dramatic effects and feel the challenge to walk up those hills in that penetrating wind.

Moreover, a farm was not the place for me. There were the cries of animals being killed and, worst of all, the spaniel dog was terribly thrashed for supposedly killing chickens which it was later found were being attacked by a vicious pig. I trust the family made it up later to the dog for this case of mistaken identity.

It therefore seemed quite a miracle when we descended from these dramatic heights to the brilliant sunshine of a summer day at Aberdovey. I shall never forget that day because neither Nanny nor I had ever seen the sea before and we shared the wonderment of this new experience. The sun has never seemed so brilliant nor the sand so golden as on that heavenly afternoon. What an amazing sight that great area of sparkling blue water was and the waves that washed in round one's feet in such a fascinating manner such as I had never seen before. Clad in what we should now think far too many clothes, with a special pair of large size stiff paddling knickers and apron to contain all these, I took a great liking to the water which has lasted all my life. It is curious that although I took after my father in most things, I shared my mother's love of the sea and my brother, like my father, preferred the mountains.

We returned again and again to it for bathes, even starting the day with one before breakfast, but the latter expedition proved too much for me one morning and I turned sick. So Nanny had to divert my attention while Mummy and Daddy and Ralph slipped out to the beach. I recall one morning I caught them coming in and was most indignant that I had not been allowed to participate.

We stayed at Trefedian Terrace a little way out of the town, with a lovely sitting room with a bow window looking out towards the sea. As happens in all those Welsh coast towns the railway runs between the houses and the beach. There was a family joke about how Nanny thinking she had got right away from industrial north Staffordshire and the collieries which she so disliked, looked out of the window on that first morning and saw, to her disgust, a whole string of coal trucks labelled 'Foxfield Colliery' passing the sitting room window. This was the main colliery at Dilhorne.

When you reached the beach there were lovely sand dunes – another unusual sight for me. Glorious Holly Blue butterflies were fluttering about on the blue thistles and sparse vegetation in the sheltered folds. As it was such a quiet beach one did not have to go through the awful ceremony of undressing in bathing machines, so strictly enforced in those days on town beaches, but one found privacy and also warmth in some cosy dip in the dunes. But of course they had no numbers for identification on them.

There was one alarming occasion when we came out of the sea, probably having drifted down the beach somewhat, and we could not find the dune we had undressed in. My mother got frantic for fear we should catch cold – in those days sunbathing in your costume when you came out of the water was unheard of. Neither propriety nor the tradition to keep fully clothed and warm permitted it. She rushed up to an astonished lady and said urgently:

'Can you tell us where we have come from?'

Flying saucers and interplanetary travel were not talked of then or she might have suspected us of being bewildered visitors from Mars.

My father brought Rover tickets on the railway – Runabouts I think they were called – and we steamed up and down the coast on the old Cambrian Railway, exploring a new place almost every day, Barmouth, Harlech, we got to know them all, but what I remember best was the delight of being put down by the boat on 'Shell Island' and gazing at the soft pink mountain of shells in brilliant sunshine and feeling the warm mass scrunching under my feet. Of course, there were so many lovely treasures to gather up we brought many back and used to gaze at the delicate colouring and tinted interiors with amazement.

We have some amusing photos taken on those trips, mostly on the beach – my mother in extraordinarily long skirts and wearing her one extravagance in those days, a large Woodrow hat. My father is still attired in his clerical garb with his hard black straw hat on but he has rolled up his clerical trousers to enable him to paddle with us in the sea. What a contrast to these days when even Father Superiors in Rome wear fishermen jerseys and open white cricket shirts.

It was not only naturalist souvenirs from Wales that we brought back with us. Nanny, thinking of her mother Nanniemigger and other members of her family who would expect little gifts from Wales, in those days an almost far-away land, took us to the local souvenir shop. It was kept by a very Welsh lady who spoke in a rather slow voice, which enabled Nanny to pick up the tune of her Welsh accent and typical expressions and amuse us by quoting them at home later.

What I enjoyed most in the shop was the discovery of the Welsh costume with its glorious chimney hat and white wimple inside. It seemed to have a fairy-story like quality, to me. I was very pleased when the family bought various souvenirs and we took back images of it on biscuit tins and handkerchiefs which appeared in the nursery.

We had discovered a wonderful new land.

VII

The World of Adults

The Germans did not invade Hixon as I had anticipated, but the invasion of Belgium was to bring vast changes into my life. For us a financial crisis began, because prices rocketed – even eggs cost a shilling each *if* you could get them. My father's stipend still remained at the modest level of under £300 per year. His war work helping with the visiting in a big parish in the Potteries caused him extra expense. He received little or no remuneration for this. My parents therefore decided that they must cut down expenses in all directions, this included giving up their whole staff except for a man in the garden an odd few hours each week. Nanny's mother was somewhat ageing at this time and needed a daughter at home, so by mutual consent she left us, to devote herself to someone else who needed taking care of. Truly her vocation has seemed to be service to others all her life. I do not recall there was any heartbreaking parting from Nanny. We loved her too dearly to ever lose touch and I constantly went to stay in her little cottage on the borders of Shropshire, the only place I would go to without my mother.

I suppose I did have a great affection for my mother also, because she, with her practical gifts, had participated actively in family life and never became a remote figure like some mothers who kept a Nanny. I think I wanted both Nanny and Mummy but in quite different ways, sometimes both at the same time, as I recall from an amusing episode that must have happened when I was very young.

Nanny had been on holiday and got back after I had gone to bed. My mother therefore had taken on the duty of sitting by me until I went to sleep. I was dozing off when I noticed sleepily that Nanny had appeared on the scene and she and

Mummy were whispering together, prior to Mummy handing over to Nanny. I felt against the idea of Mummy departing so I decided to keep them both. I started to cry, therefore, directly I saw Mummy prepare to go. Rather than have a crisis and have me awake for some time I suppose, my mother gave in and sat down again hoping I would soon be asleep. I then took up a rather owl-like pose appearing to close my eyes but peeping out of a corner of one of them. Directly I perceived any movement on my mother's or Nanny's part I set up a further hullabaloo and they were obliged to sit down again till I was really sound asleep.

Life had taken on a very different shape for my mother now. By and large, I think she really enjoyed looking after us herself, and she also appreciated the new social attitude to such things. It appealed to her love of the unconventional. She used to laugh and say:

'Before the war came people would have looked askance at me scrubbing my own doorstep – but now what does it matter,' she would add triumphantly.

The dismissal of our servants meant a change for us also. The centre of my life was no longer the nursery but the dining room. I began to take part much more in adult life, and observe the activities of the parish. Many and varied people came and went into the big dining room while I was playing in it because it was the centre of my father's work. His study, where it should have been done, was by the front door and too cold to use most of the year. There was a smell of mustiness in keeping with the pale sepia copy of a famous picture of St John the Baptist, and brown slightly mouldy books in an old bookcase. These are my chief memories of it.

My father did his work at a large oak desk in the dining room in a sunny corner by the window, looking out on to the lawn. It was topped by a tall bookcase which contained large sized editions of Scott in leather covers and other classics. But the books that were the most exciting for me were the five volumes of Lydekker's Natural History books. I used to delve into these with delight. Like most Victorian books the pictures were heavily 'furnished' with every detail. I used to gaze at the coloured pictures of tropical snakes in their natural habitat until I felt that I was walking in that forest in reality.

There was a large overmantel by the fireplace, with carved oak columns at the side. Some nice bits of Staffordshire china stood on it that Daddy had picked up cheap at junk shops as you did in those days. There were brass spill cups for his pipe cleaners and most important of all, a large rack to hold his pipes. This object seemed very much to the fore in these latter days when I was beginning to take in more about adult things. It was here on the hearth that visitors of importance used to stand, pipe in mouth, clad in breeches or later plus fours, and make manly pronouncements on the situation in the country or sometimes the world. To these we all listened in those days with respectful attention.

The chairs were basket ones of the type known as Varsity, probably so-called because they originated in college rooms, and they were brought back by young curates intending to settle down. They were tub-shaped and quite upright at the back, they had none of the reclining luxury of the modern chair, but their severity was padded by the addition of cushions. Ours were held in place by loose covers made by Nanny in a William Morris pattern material of tropical grasses and peacocks, the facsimile of which I recently saw in an exhibition at the Victoria and Albert Museum.

My own special corner of the room where I used to play when people called was against an oak sideboard behind the door. This piece of furniture was particularly famous because of the youthful sallies that my brother used to make to it as a toddler, in order to take the stoppers out of the whisky decanter and others and lick them. He discovered the low cupboard was within his reach and thought it a great joke, but a maiden aunt who saw him doing it evinced alarm for his future, but actually Ralph grew up a rather more temperate person than most young men.

I do not recall that these receptacles which were little more than social accoutrements and seldom brought out caught my own imagination much. My memory of that corner is mostly of a very large picture which covered the whole wall of the alcove in which the sideboard stood. It was a romantic scene of a man and woman in long robes gazing at each other in a rather decorated rowing boat enclosed romantically in trees and other vegetation. It created another world to look in on.

There were, of course, some occasions when visitors arrived and I was immediately whisked away to the kitchen or some other temporary centre for my activities, for my father was noted for his kindness and sympathy so people felt encouraged to come and consult him about their problems. There were, constantly shy young men sitting on the edge of their chairs who had obviously come to put the banns up, I soon learnt, but there were more permanent and complicated people such as old ''Er says and 'er says.' She gained this rather extraordinary title in our family vocabulary because of her habit of reeling off in detail perpetual arguments she had with her sister with whom she shared the house. As she mumbled terribly my father could never follow all these, and it really did not seem to matter, so long as she had a sympathetic ear. But his hearing got quite attune to the oft repeated chorus ''er says and I says' so that he could put in a few sympathetic nods here. The sign that the long disquisition was nearing its end came however, when she sat back and repeated, fervently, to impress my father, no doubt, by this biblical utterance, 'Ah, well, with the help of my God I will yet leap over the wall.'

How thankfully he heard the sound of this grand finale, to which his ears had become sufficiently accustomed to pick it out from the verbal mêlée, knowing he would now be released to go back to his Sunday sermon, which was often lying half finished on his desk.

There were other well meaning but embarrassing ladies who disrupted the family menage somewhat. There was, for instance, Mrs Putt, a sturdy lady who came one day to the Church with her married daughter to get the baby christened. They had walked all the way from Godley Brook, an outlying part, in a snowstorm, so naturally my father took them back to the Vicarage to tea where my mother welcomed them.

The baby, no doubt a little disturbed by the upheavals of its usual routine on this great occasion, started to yell lustily. Its grandmother, extremely anxious that it should not misbehave on such an occasion, took the baby's dummy out, thoroughly licked it herself first, and then to our horror plunged it wet into the sugar basin on the table, which contained the whole of our war-time ration for a week. She then stuffed it in the baby's mouth.

Unfortunately, this treatment only brought temporary relief and the process was repeated many times before the tea party ended. As my mother said afterwards as she consigned a good portion of it to the dustbin, if only Mrs Putt had been content to only let the baby lick it I would not have minded!

There were, however, rare occasions when, perhaps through the justice of providence, we were the recipients rather than the givers. This certainly was so in the case of Miss Brassington, a parishioner in a lonely farm on the hillside above the parish. She was a bespectacled lady with a rosy complexion. She had the modesty of a suburban spinster, which blended in a curious way with the rugged courage and realism of the northern farm working family.

She was a great admirer of my father, and during the hungry days of the First World War, her devotion found practical expression. Under cover of darkness, she would slip down to the Vicarage with a wicker basket covered with an immaculate white cloth. I can see her now, coming into the brightly-lit dining room, blinking over her gold-rimmed spectacles, clad in old-fashioned faded black. She never seemed to wear any modern coloured clothes or even rough tweeds like the other womenfolk did. There she would sit, usually on an upright chair at the huge oak table, and after a little preliminary chatter, she would unwrap the immaculate white table napkin and lay her treasures on the table. They were a glowing, yellow entourage, as fresh as dew, baskets of flowers in miniature, shells and all kinds of culinary objets d'art, all wrought in the frail medium of dairy butter.

They were supposed to be brought specially for me because I was considered delicate, but I very much suspect they were really given out of admiration for my father. I was encouraged to consume some of the smaller tit-bits, such as the basket of flowers, on the spot. My mother always said about any food she thought good in those days, 'Oh eat it, it's so nourishing.' My brother always said that that was enough to damn any food straight off. As I had not acquired his schoolboy contempt for nourishment as something 'cissy', I responded to the invitation to consume them with uninhibited alacrity.

How well I remember the delight of popping these enchanting toys into my mouth, and feeling them melt into a soft nothingness, leaving only that salty tang peculiar to real farmhouse butter. Certainly it seemed a literal demonstration of the frailty of beauty.

These were only embellishments to the real context of the basket, however, for there were always one or two half pounds, done up in blocks, with neatly bevelled edges, which were put on the stone slab in the larder to provide a regular supply for some time ahead.

Miss Brassington was the champion butter-maker of the county actually. It used to puzzle us, when we saw the old-fashioned kitchen at the farm, how she attained to such heights. I have come to see, however, that she was in a sense the true artist, an individual who worked best in her own characteristic surroundings. She would never have done well in a stereotyped, streamlined kitchen, the mecca of most housewives today.

Miss Brassington had a most amusing old father – a striking Falstaffian figure of about eighty, extremely fat, with a long white beard. He was something of a wag, enjoying the gaieties of life as he envisaged them, and very fond of his glass at the pub. There was a story told of how, returning up the Hall back drive one night, full of exuberance after visiting the Wheatsheaf, he met the rather prim governess from the Hall, and chucked her under the chin, in spite of the fact that she backed into a roadside gutter to avoid his advances. He certainly chose a most unfortunate subject for his spontaneous demonstration of affection because it caused her great consternation.

His English was rather basic, and permeated of course by local dialect. There was a story told of how the doctor called on him once during his last years, and was pleased to see the old man had improved. Shouting into what he hoped was his best ear, he reported, 'Well, Mr Brassington, you are better than you were.' This statement, however, was greeted with a look of complete incomprehension. Marshalling his strength again, the doctor bellowed, 'You are better than you were.' Still there was a questioning look on the old man's face. Then his rosy-cheeked daughter stepped in.

'Eh, father,' she said in soft tones, 'Doctor says yer better than yer *was*.'

A look of instant comprehension lit up the old man's face. 'Oh, eie,' he said, 'I'm better than I *was*.'

Certainly his command of the English language, and appropriate phrases, were very adaptive. He recounted to my father an interview purported to have taken place between our dowager squiress and her agent who was a very severe lady something like Queen Victoria. The matter under discussion was that of Brassington taking over another of her farms. Her Ladyship was apparently so enthusiastic about the suggested tenant that, according to him, she said, 'Let Brassington have it. Man taks 'is coat off to it'!

The old man did not, as far as I can remember, ever call on us at the Vicarage, but I visited the farm because I had now begun to accompany my parents on parish visits as there was no one to leave me with.

This necessity to take me with them produced rather a problem as regards distant visits. My father called on every house in the village once a year, often accompanied by my mother. But many of these were in outlying parts, where a bicycle or pram was only an encumbrance, and walking seemed the only solution. This presented a big problem as I was only able to walk a moderate distance, and too heavy to be carried.

Then quite suddenly a solution presented itself, due really to a tragic happening in the parish. Our farmer friends, to whom we later gave the pony Merrylegs, had a donkey which they had bought for their own daughter Connie. She was an only and much adored child who, at the age of eight years, suddenly died.

It was the first time I can recall realising that anyone died. I suppose I must have heard of someone else, some old person perhaps, but it had never registered in my mind before. It did not, as far as I can recall, mean any great personal loss for me because I had only once seen Connie when we called at the farm and then in the distance. But I can remember Nanny's surprise and dismay when she heard the child was dead, and how she and Mummy talked about the event in shocked tones. It transpired that she had had an operation, for T.B. glands, done at home, as they were in those days, by the family doctor and a visiting surgeon. Connie survived the operation but died later from chloroform poisoning.

I remember feeling impressed and puzzled by the fact that someone could suddenly die like this and felt this was a new problem to fit into my scheme of things.

As she was an only child the parents were terribly distressed (and I regret to say they never had another), so they were only too glad to find a good home for her pet donkey Jinnie where another little girl could ride her.

We must have inherited an old side saddle with her, and my parents, again wishing to pad the corners of my life, I suppose, did not have me taught to ride independently, but let me ride astride clinging on to the pommel on the saddle.

Gripping hold of this large object gave me a great sense of stability until one day, when I happened to be what seemed to me an alarming distance away from my parents, I realised my angle of gravitation had gone completely out of line. Vainly I clutched at the pommel, normally my source of security, but I realised that gradually my whole world was turning upside down, and the surface of the road coming towards me. I shrieked for help. Luckily my parents heard my cries and rushed forward to rescue me. My mother swept me up into her arms while my father tightened the girths, the source of trouble, and my oscillating world. Even in their anxiety they could not help roaring with laughter at my predicament. I remember feeling deeply offended at this, like every other over-protected child. I wanted such an unpleasant experience to be taken very seriously.

Jinnie was most useful when we visited the moorland farms high up above the main parish, especially in winter, when the task was more rigorous. The parish was itself divided into districts, with differing people and customs. What they all had in common was a certain hardy independence, characteristic of north country folk. This made them difficult to know at first. It took my father five years to escape the label of 'foreigner'. After that, 'Parson Plant', as the old moorland farmers called him (the a's pronounced very soft, as is the custom in the north), was accepted in every home.

Whenever there is an east wind blowing, and the winter trees stand out on the hilltops stark against a red sky, I am reminded of parish visiting. With what zest we climbed the winding road to the upper part known simply as 'Bank Top' until we came to where the fields were no longer encircled by sheltering hedges such as we knew at home, but mapped out like a chess board with grey stone walls. As we got higher, the wind blew keener in our faces, and we felt braced to the task, moving the faster to keep warm.

On the way up, we often turned aside from the road and staggered along some muddy cart track, through untidy woods, to visit some lonely house cut off from the ordinary world.

It was often late before we completed our rounds, and darkness came on. Then my father would light his old brass storm lantern containing a single candle. By its light we blundered across the humpy fields and into the muddy farmyards, where barking dogs and men with lanterns came out of the cowsheds to greet us.

'Yer can go in. Yer will find the Missis at home,' they would say, in friendly fashion, feeling their social attributes inadequate, but glad someone was there to welcome us.

Then we would turn to the back door, picking our way carefully through a medley of pails and churns, to be welcomed by 'the Missis'. She usually came to the door in heavy nailed boots, that clamped harshly on the cold blue bricks, and wore a sacking apron over her heavy tweed clothes. The farmhouses were not of the cosy, romantic type, like those in the south or west, but grey and severe, in keeping with the hard life of the folk who lived in them.

We were always taken into the kitchen for a chat, a cosy, over-crowded room, smelling of old clothes and sides of bacon, which hung on great hooks over our heads. The beautifully kept parlours were too cold to enter. I cannot recall ever penetrating into them even in summer for more than a brief period, to glance at a family photograph, and to inspect some supposed art treasure. One wondered for what purpose they were used other than as a place to keep the Sunday hats belonging to the women of the family. These familiar landmarks in church were usually laid carefully on the table or dresser as soon as they got home, like a bishop's mitre, awaiting the next festival when custom permitted they should be worn.

It was snug sitting by the roaring fire in the kitchen, in spite of the conglomeration of draughts the houses were subject to. The grate was always the old iron kitchener type, with its oven on one side, and the boiler with a tap on the other.

If there was an older member of the family, they would be sitting by the fire in an upright ladder backed chair. People reached a great age up there on the top. I particularly recall one tough old lady who lived alone in a small farm until she was 100. She fascinated us children because she had a nut-cracker face like a witch, and a heavy beard. There was one occasion when I went up to take her, and a neighbouring farmer, to the poll in my car. He was a hardy, jolly man. As we passed his home on the way down the hill, with the old lady sitting up beside him, weird and severe in her bonnet, he leant out of the window and called out to his little daughter,

'Tell yer mother I'm going to get married again!'

My father was always in despair about the old woman because she kept her dog perpetually chained, and to a most inadequate kennel. Again and again he spoke to her about it, but she was quite unrelenting. She would take no notice. That was one of the black spots in the local tradition. Farm dogs were seldom let loose, so different to the tradition of the sheep farms north west, where they had long spells of exercise, and then slept in barns. In our district they were fastened up in the yard, often to small, leaking kennels, and on short chains. When you went to the house, they came out at you with a roar. They often became so fierce with frustration that it was unsafe to let them loose at all. Even the nicer owners did little about it because they were embedded in traditional behaviour, and they simply could not view the situation objectively. That is one of the reasons why I can never feel, like many people, that the country is a peaceful heaven on earth, where the mind can be at rest. Later I came to feel so much happier among plump suburban dogs, and the East Ender's fat, urbane cats, individual members of the family compared to the hungry herd of starving farm cats, and the fierce, chained collies.

It was here, on the top of the hill, that the haunted house stood. It was a large, sinister-looking place outside, with peeling plaster walls, and big sash windows. My father took a great interest in such things, and always collected any local ghost stories he could. We were not to know then, how valuable this interest in psychic matters would be in a crisis later in our family life.

The story told about this house was that a door in the corridor dividing the front and back hall was always swinging open. It would not remain shut even when locked. Several different residents corroborated the story, and one of them described to my father how he lay in bed and heard steps coming up the stairs and right up to the side of his bed. He saw the chair there beside the bed rocking to and fro in the moonlit room as the invisible steps shook the floor.

On investigating the history of the house, my father found that a long time ago a farmer had lived there, whose daughter fell in love with a man he did not approve of. He forbade her to see him, but one day, when the young man thought the father would be away at market, he decided to call on her. On his way up to the farm, he stopped at the local public house, called the Wagon and Horses to have a drink. He mentioned his destination to someone then. That was the last time he was ever seen alive – for he mysteriously disappeared after that. For some reason, the matter never appears to have been investigated, so it remains entirely unsolved. In more recent years, the floor of the corridor by the haunted door collapsed. The farmer had the subsidence filled in. My father was very sorry he would not have it excavated. He thought they would probably find the young man's body there, and if it was given Christian burial, the ghost might be liberated.

Just beyond this house, where two main roads forked, stood a Nonconformist chapel, one of those severe-looking conventicles typical of the north. It had been plastered a pallid grey, which the hard weather had turned green. Outside the chapel stood a big board, on which it was customary to put a challenging text. Having exhausted all the most orthodox ones, the supporters decided to go in for a real piece of Hot Gospelling, and painted up in large letters:

'Are you sure of your Road to Eternity?'

The sturdy farming folk were quite unintimidated by this fearful challenge, and merely transferred the title to the bus stop nearby. Long after the fiery words had paled and faded from the notice board, the name for the bus stop remained. Many a tired housewife, returning home from market laden with baskets and mewling children, would sink thankfully into her seat, murmuring with all the assurance of a space traveller, 'One whole and two halves to Eternity, please.'

VIII

Local Personalities

We descended from this bleak moorland land into a belt of trees and bigger farms on the valley side.

Then gradually as we went on the vegetation got scarcer and more black and stunted until it almost disappeared. Then the whole scene was dominated by the great black colliery tips, which stood up above us like long barren mountains diffusing a queer chemical smell whenever they caught fire. Yet their long greyness, and their strange odour, remembered particularly in the cold autumn air, will be something that will remain dear to many I think who have lived in the colliery north.

At the very bottom of the hill where the road divided into two, there was a hamlet called Godley Brook. There was little godly about it. It was made up of bleak, red-brick cottages, with inadequate accommodation, a memorial to the industrial revolution, when anything was considered good enough for the worker's home.

The brook, too, was a rather meandering, meagre affair, but where it went under a tiny bridge, where the two roads met, a pair of Nonconformist chapels had been built, which may have been the origin of the name. They were very early Victorian buildings, built like the cottages, of small red brick, but with some stone embellishments to make them more impressive, the whole heavily discoloured by years of smoke from the pit. They were served mostly by lay preachers, who travelled round the circuit. My father was on very good terms with the chapels, and since they had to use the graveyard at the church for burials, he often shared the funeral in the church with the Minister who was generally called in on these special occasions from a chapel in a nearby town. There was quite a lot of dual attendance by the parishioners of both places of worship. Many of our church attenders used to disappear on certain Sundays. They had gone to support the chapels at a yearly activity, which went by the fascinating name of 'The Sittings Up'.

Of course, inevitably, there was in this small hamlet, a public house. It was a respectable sort of place, and was primarily, I think, a centre for the men to get a break from the hard life of the pit, and the overcrowded surroundings at home. The pub was kept by a man and his wife we knew well, called Sales. He himself worked also as a miner. He was called up during the First World War and badly wounded. I always recall going with my mother in the pony trap to fetch him from the station when he was invalided home with a badly injured leg and how he said to my mother so fervently his great sorrow was that, owing to his injury, he would never be able to work in the pit again. Actually, his leg did get completely better, and he lived to fulfil his wish. It seems strange to think that within a few years, the next generation were coming home from yet another war but they were saying, 'The one thing I am grateful to this war for is freeing me from the colliery. I've made up my mind that I'll *never* go down the pit again.'

The road from Godley Brook led up a steep hill past the school to the centre of the village where there was a shop and another pub. A great many of our friends belonging to the mining community lived up a funny little side road known as 'Sarver Lane'.

The houses were typical of the miners' dwellings, but they did not have the usual drawback of being back to back. Some of them had good gardens, which they kept very well.

Inside, however, they had absolutely none of the amenities considered essential today. There was usually only one proper bedroom, the second consisting only of a landing. Here a large double bed was placed for most of the children to pile into. The floor area was so small that part of it had to be placed dangerously near the staircase, with only a very inadequate rail to prevent anyone rolling out of bed and crashing downstairs in the night.

There was no fireplace or other means of heating upstairs,

and no water. There was no pre-natal care or maternity hospital accommodation, so all babies were born at home, and usually delivered in the family living room in order to have warmth and water. Even then the latter had to be carried from a waterhouse. The same arrangements were often made when someone got very ill in winter. It had the asset too of keeping the patient handy for the neighbours who might be acting as part-time nurses, but it gave the patient little quiet and privacy. Certainly the whole family got a very realistic picture of the details of life and death in those days.

Though everyone was very poor, the miners and their families did everything to make the best of their homes. As coal was the one plentiful thing they had, there was always a roaring fire to welcome you. When we called in the late afternoon, high tea was generally in progress. It was held when the children came home from school, and the menfolk were no longer 'in their dirt', as the thick covering of coal dust was called. They came home from the pit with it still on in those days as there were no pithead baths. An unsuspecting maiden aunt when paying us a visit one day remarked to my father, 'What a lot of sweeps you have got in your parish, George. I met a whole group of them coming down the road just now!'

On entering the miner's living room, we were usually asked in a welcoming voice to 'sit yerselves down'. This we did, usually on a horsehair sofa, which was inevitably under the window, and nearly always covered with cotton of a red Paisley design.

The big brown teapot stewing on the hob, an important but dreaded weapon of hospitality, was then seized up, and several more teaspoonfuls added in our honour, though it was far too strong already. Tea drinking was as inescapable a rite as coffee is in the Middle East, but you needed a very strong stomach to withstand its effects.

Conversation ranged round the doings of the family and their neighbours, and provided a series of colourful vignettes expressed with telling directness in rich, northern voices, which gave them character of their own.

'Oh, 'ee ain't arf a one for havin' a run round the Pottery', – an allusion to a neighbour who was in the habit of going too

Ralph dressed in a traditional sailor suit and myself

Left: With Nanny and Ralph by the walnut tree

Below: Nanny and her sister Tippo

often to the dazzling Mecca of the Five Towns. Someone else had 'gone clerical', meaning she had raised herself to the standard of the black-coated worker, considered an unfortunate social promotion to a realistic mining family. 'Stuck up, that's what she is now. I would not like my girl to go clerical.'

Two other local residents were said to be 'goshawking' too much. On looking in the dictionary, I found that appropriately enough a goshawk is a kind of hawk that frequently utters strange croaking noises.

Anything which failed to come up to the acid test as they applied it was generally dismissed with the descriptive sentence of 'Not much bottle'.

In spite of these restrictive conditions, making life a vital struggle for most of the miners' families, many of them were happy. They were a realistic people who adapted their way of life to suit their conditions.

One of our friends in the centre of the village was a large, cumbersome lady who managed to bring up fourteen children in the type of one-room upstairs plus a landing I have just described. Only once did she lose one of her brood. He was found about a mile away heading towards the railway station at a very tender age. His mother said apologetically to the authorities who questioned her about his escape, 'I'm sorry he over got me'. It was amazing that more things did not overget her in such conditions.

In those days it was the fashion in the village to dress children up to about three years old in skirts whatever their sex, and provide no nether garments. This saved a great deal of trouble on washday, but left the children quite unprotected from the rigours of the cold northern air. My mother used to be horrified when she saw them sitting with their bare skin on cold stone doorsteps for hours.

But perhaps her sense of balance, and a reminder that a child is very adaptable, and each mother makes her own standards, came when this mother of fourteen came late one evening at the Vicarage to see some rummage. She was most alarmed when she saw we slept with our bedroom windows wide open. 'Eh,' she exclaimed in horror, 'my children would be fair clemmed if I let 'em sleep like that.'

'Clemmed' is the dialect word for 'cold' in Staffordshire as it is in low German too, I believe, strangely enough.

From the centre of the village the road passed on to Church End, built between the church and the front entrance to the Hall. Here the houses became cosier and more individual, and the atmosphere more restrained. The élite of the village, such as the old Hall servants, lived here. Hitched on to the coachman's cottage at an angle, as if discreetly looking the other way, was Ivy Cottage, where the retired housekeeper and her sister lived. The steps to the door were perpetually white, the garden immaculately neat. It seemed a long way from the miners' homes, by the dark slag-heaps hidden away conveniently by a hill. But sometimes, when the wind was in the north, the sound of the familiar whirr of the hedgestocks invaded the garden, like the throbbings of a double bass below the more delicate strings in an orchestra.

At Ivy Cottage, tea was not offered us as in other homes, not through lack of hospitality but because of different social custom. The pot was not left standing on the hob perpetually here, and even if it had been, it would not have been considered good manners to invite the gentry to partake of it in this haphazard way. I remember once going to tea there by special invitation, and it was a ceremony almost as intricate as a Chinese one. It was served in the best parlour, with much-treasured china brought out for the occasion, polished and shining like silver. The cakes were of the most delicate home-made variety, made by the eldest Miss Bolton who had been the housekeeper at the Hall.

From long practice in service the sisters had acquired the most discreet professional voices. The effort of hearing what they said when they reached the climax of a story added greatly to its interest value. Even the most legitimate baby was made to seem excitingly scandalous when its advent was heralded by them in whispers; whilst the Misses Bolton's own sorties to a neighbouring market town took on the picturesqueness of the Grand Tour when crystallised into such delicious phrases as, 'We alighted at Leek.'

In the cottage next door allotted to the retired Hall coachman and his wife, lived our most beloved friend among all the village folk, Mrs Thornton. Of Irish origin, she had a natural dignity and good looks as well as a spiritual beauty. Her face was oval, and her skin delicate and fine, and her eyes were extraordinarily steadfast and kindly. But like most great souls, she had a twinkling sense of humour. Her familiar comment 'That's rich', when one told her an amusing tale, became a household word. When I went to Norway in later life, I met several old ladies with a definite resemblance to her. Coming to know more of Norwegian history, I saw how her unusual type of good looks was due possibly to traces of Norwegian ancestry as well as Irish, since the Vikings occupied Ireland for so long and inter-married.

Mrs Thornton was the only person, I think, whom we took right inside our family circle. So high was our opinion of her that my mother used to say, 'If Mrs Thornton ever turned out false, I should never believe in anyone again.'

After Nanny left, my mother had great difficulty in leaving me with anyone while she went out. I was so used to having either her or Nanny with me, I had hysterics with strangers. But Mrs Thornton was different. I suppose I identified her as part of the family so there seemed no cause to feel insecure or shy. When she and I were alone together for a long day in the big old Vicarage, it always seemed safe. When it got dusk and *she* lit the lamp, not just because she had been her ladyship's parlourmaid before her marriage and knew how to handle such things deftly, but because she created such quiet and peace, the event went off without any upset. How the governesses I used to have shrieked and dithered when they did it, cracked the chimney because they put it on crooked and then let the thing flame up, while I stood by in terror. Mrs Thornton seemed to spread peace and quiet over everything, until the travellers returned, and the house was full of people again, as I was used to it being normally.

Mrs Thornton was very adaptable too. She was perfectly ready to play all kinds of games. What fun we had dressing up in the rummage which was temporarily lodged with us by the Squiress and other benefactors for the next Parish Sale.

I remember on one occasion the Hall governess sent us the most wonderful black net skirt of endless frills, which had belonged to her mother. Mrs Thornton donned this with great success for some play I arranged. She was tall and dignified, and it suited her perfectly. Hardly had she done so, however, and was making up the old-fashioned grate to keep us warm, when a heavy thundering began on the front door. We realised with alarm that this must be Cynthia, the Squire's daughter. She would doubtless be accompanied by her governess, the donor of the skirt.

For once Mrs Thornton quite lost her usual composure at this embarrassing situation. She had practised the stewardship of other people's belongings so assiduously in her professional life. And here she was implicated in wearing one without having asked the owner first. Hastening too much to complete the stoking operation and take off the garment before opening the door, she got the guard entangled irretrievably in the frills. Further thunderings on the door announced the visitor's childish impatience to be admitted to the house immediately, where she knew she was normally always welcome at any moment.

There was no time to be lost. The only way out of the difficulty was to strip off the skirt and bury the guard and the foaming yards of net behind a cushion in one of the long 'varsity' chairs.

We then guiltily admitted our guests. But imagine our consternation when Miss Gold, the governess, as if attracted by some magnetic power, sat down on the very chair where it was hidden, and proceeded to pat the cushion into shape. After eyeing her nervously, and carrying on absent-minded conversations with both of them, we were forced to give up the subterfuge, which fitted us both so badly, and confess to the dreadful truth. Luckily our visitors were delighted at the joke, and the offending objects were retrieved, and with much careful co-operation by all four of us, disentangled from their tortuous embrace.

I used to visit the Thorntons' house sometimes when my mother wanted to get me out of the way. Their front door was encircled by a wonderful clematis, from which the house took its name, flanked in patches of purple montbretia which grew over stones at each side of the door. Inside it was full of knick-knacks fascinating for a child to see, from a case full of stuffed birds to an exquisite old musical box which stood under the window. What a thrill it was when she turned it on, the delicate minuet-like notes seemed the perfect background to her charm, like an old lilac print.

Across the lane that ran up to the farm by their house, the Thorntons' proper garden lay. It was approached by a wicket gate and up some stone steps. On the left there was a seat which was set against the wall of their neighbour's cow shed. It was sheltered therefore and warm too because it faced towards the sun. There she and Thornton used to sit very upright, with a strange placid dignity, almost akin to royalty but one which sprang from a natural attunement to their life rather than a conditioned schooling of court manners.

Thornton was clean shaven with a thin pink face. He wore a collar which always fascinated me. It was rather like a very high clerical one, but with an almost invisible cross-over at the front. Below it he had a padded stock of clear blue, with an immaculate tie pin in the middle of it. This was, I suppose, a relic of his younger days when he drove out sitting proudly upright on the coachman's box.

The garden was shared with a family called Madeley who lived on the other side of it just by the Parish Room. It was a tribute to their good neighbourliness that there was no dividing hedge. Mr Madeley was my father's Churchwarden, a striking-looking man, very tall with white hair that waved off his temples. His weekday occupation was winder at the pit, a job of considerable responsibility of course. I don't think that I ever thought of him as the instigator of the turning hedgestocks and that strange whirring noise that went on night and day in the distance. It was too impersonal and symbolic to me to have so simple and direct a human agent involved in its process.

Mrs Madeley was a plump, virile little woman who always wore small gold ear-rings which were the perfect counterpart to her gay rather cockney spice. My father used to love to chaff her. One day he gave her a lift to the station in the pony trap and announced that he was on his way to meet two ladies who were coming to stay. At this she pricked up her ears, being always glad to be first with the local news. They were coming to stay for a long time, my father added, which heightened her interest. Then he added they were going to live in the loft at the top of the building by the dog house. For a moment she looked at him, bewildered, then sensing a leg-pull she rapped out in her quick north country voice, 'Ah no ladies them!' She was right. They happened to be two beagles my father was adding to his already large flock.

Mrs Madeley was the Church Keeper and cleaner, and when I encounter the smell of many flowers in a cool church a picture of her will always come back to me. Not the romantic and delicate smell of a few choice blooms in the sanctuary, but banks of them on altars and window sills with piles of stalks and waste greenery lying on the floor, and helpers moving around arranging them. Through this floral bustle and chaos Mrs Madeley would come chasing a few delinquent blooms back into the main pile with her broom. She would pause as she passed you and utter a few laconic words which indicated she could a tale unfold, and if you followed this up by the right responses you would hear some interesting piece of village news she was longing to impart.

Nearly opposite the Madeleys lived the Chadwicks, the family of our late schoolmaster. There were seven of them and all were gifted in music in some way. They were the lynch pin of the choir, in fact of the whole church. All the thirty years my father was vicar, while other parishioners came and went through the years, losing interest in the church or taking umbrage at some imaginary tiff, the Chadwicks stayed on, a devoted and immovable foundation stone to things. They were a sort of eternal land-mark in the front pews on Sunday where the women's choir sat. I can still remember the variations in hats that they had, especially at Easter, when new Easter bonnets seemed an essential innovation. I still recall a pale blue satin Topper which seemed to reach an amazing height, and which appeared one year and caused quite a sensation, especially as it was worn by Beattie, one of the most modest of the family. My father twitted her about it and she hung her head and gave a characteristic giggle, not being quite aware herself even why she had blossomed out into this object of such prima donna-like glamour.

I have always thought it was foolish of St Paul to enjoin women to cover their heads in church, as hats can be a good deal more disturbing to devotions than heads. But then he lived in the Middle East where women veiled themselves and he had never come across the fascinating contrivance and diversion of the modern hat.

Now that Nanny had left, Christmas was no longer spent in the nursery but downstairs among the pastoral activities of a parson's family. The advent of Christmas precipitated a great amount of work for us. At 6 a.m. my father would start his church services, which went on mostly until lunch time. My mother had many gifts to take around. She was the kind of parson's wife who hated attending committee meetings but delighted in looking after people who were ill, cooking them tempting dishes, or sitting up with them at night whilst the relatives took some rest. In those days there were very few hospitals and an illness often placed a very heavy burden on a family.

During Christmas dinner we discussed all the news about the parish. My father would talk of the total number of communicants he had had, sometimes it was many, sometimes too few. All of them had been bidden by a special Christmas Communion card. There were always surprises about who responded to this and who did not.

There was much talk about those who were home for Christmas especially in the big families, like the retired schoolmaster's or the Hall coachman's, whom we knew so well. Of course, someone was nearly always absent in each family circle. A married child had gone to in-laws, or could not leave work long enough to make the journey home worthwhile. These gaps always worried me, so strong was my sense of a personal world that must be wholly complete, one in which there was no loneliness, no vacant place at the table. It upset my feeling of security to think that some were missing. I longed for a Christmas when *everyone* was there, so that my mind could rest on a completed pattern.

On Christmas afternoon, when all the services were over, and we had opened our presents, we always went to a party at our doctor's some miles away. It was in a beautiful Georgian house, with period furniture. I remember the thrill I felt on entering it. The doctor's wife was very elegant. She came of an Anglo-Indian family. She arranged everything in the home with exquisite taste. A white-walled hall led into a long drawing room, rather awe-inspiring to walk down, so we usually crept on to the sofa by the door. The floor was covered with heavy pile carpet of deep blue, the walls lined with cabinets full of beautiful china. The room ended in a bow window, draped with frilled ninon curtains and encircled by a window seat cushioned in chintz.

The sofa we generally sat on was covered in cream-coloured, silk material, with lace antimacassars. There was an enchanting red cushion, which had tiny mirrors sewn into it, and came from India.

Our hostess was, normally, a rather unhappy person. Life in this little town seemed very different to the social glamour of a British colony in India, in those days. She made a great friend of my mother, and poured out all her troubles to her, including details of the constant comings and goings of English servants whom she did not understand, during long sessions of afternoon tea. After Nanny had left us, I had to accompany my mother on these occasions. A set of Caldicott's picture books with poems like John Gilpin in them were always brought for me to read. I soon got to know these by heart, so I used to cast only a casual eye at the pages whilst listening to the extra-ordinary conversation carried on by the grown-ups. Of course, some of these things were not spoken of openly, but delicately wrapped up, or inferred, so that I should not understand them. This only increased my interest, and I worked hard to comprehend what they meant, quite often with some considerable success, as I discovered later, when I questioned my mother about them, much to her embarrassment.

On Christmas Day, however, there was a great difference. No time was wasted on these narrow, family problems. With our hostess's taste for elegance, she rose splendidly to the occasion and her husband too, with whom there were normally difficulties. The house glowed with lights and happiness. When we entered the dining room there were piles of wonderful sandwiches and cakes amidst sparkling silver, and crackers laid out on the Chippendale table. Even the servants seemed to have forgotten their grumbles and went about their duties with alacrity.

The entertainment was first-class. There were none of these artificial aids to a party such as we have now come to depend on. The only mechanised form of entertainment was a pianola, which our host played with great strength and avidity. Such a thing being a complete innovation in those days, everyone crowded round it with tremendous excitement to see the strange perforated rollers revolving rapidly in the little window above the keyboard.

A party was really a party then. Everyone worked hard to contribute to the programme. How amazing were the dual personalities, and hidden talents, that were revealed when these opportunities presented themselves! To my childish mind it was extraordinary to see dignified local doctors playing a vigorous blind man's buff, or displaying a talent for delicious backchat, or impersonations in charades. It was all the more astounding when executed in the conscientious Scottish brogue which had hitherto been associated with the solemnity of professional consultations.

The chief problem for us as a family was one of transport to the party. On our small income, we could not possibly afford a taxi. I don't recall that even in the days when we had the pony trap we ever drove out in it after dark. Luckily, as time went on all the family became great bicyclists, except myself; I was too young. But my mother solved the problem of taking me about by making a seat out of an old cushion and fixing it on the luggage carrier of her bicycle for me. By this arrangement we covered many miles. It was a very cold method of transport, however, and therefore it precluded me from wearing an ordinary thin party dress like other children. Instead, she dressed me in a white woollen jersey and pleated skirt. She was a great believer in what, I suppose, we should now call 'separates' for all occasions. As a grown up they seemed quite normal to her, but for me it meant self-consciousness and some distress as nearly everybody wore 'party frocks' in those days. I can always understand now the child who rebels against wearing a particular dress because it makes her feel odd at a party. At that age it matters so much to be one of the herd.

My first skirts were navy blue, and this attire was often much admired by the elders. I often wore a velvet band or round comb like Alice in Wonderland, to hold back my rather plain hair and I suppose it all suited my rather prim, old-fashioned style, but I myself felt like a young man who blunders into a party wearing a pullover when everyone else is in evening dress. My mother, after protests from me, changed the skirt to a white serge one which appeared more dressy, but was equally warm. But I still longed for the fluffy freedom of a real party frock.

I do not recall any English children remarking on my odd attire, they merely looked askance at me, but disaster befell me when I met a little Belgian boy a wartime refugee named Philippe.

He began his approach by pursuing me round the doctor's drawing room, crying in a high-pitched voice:

'Oh, I love you! Will you marry me?'

On being rebuffed by my stony indifference due to a British sense of propriety, he fixed his gaze on the rather unusual type of my attire. Perhaps the jersey had slipped up a little as I leaned forward to get away from him – I don't know. Anyhow, he suddenly perceived a gap between my 'separates'. As quick as lightning, he rolled my jersey up to my shoulders. To his delight he discovered underneath it a skirt bodice which, though once white looked decidedly grubby now. From then onwards he pursued me through the party wherever I went, calling out in a high pitched, squeaky voice:

'Oh, do let me see the dear little, dirty under-bodice!' and pulling up the jersey whenever he could catch up with me.

Of course, I was covered with shame, not only because the attack was amorous but even more because the bodice was dirty! He had some fat, grown-up sisters who accompanied him everywhere and whom he appeared to dislike and defy as much as possible. I remember that finally they did intervene and took him away. Needless to say, I took a dislike to foreigners after that. Perhaps it was this early experience that, unfortunately, delayed for many years my realisation when I grew up that much of my work lay in the international world, making friends with foreigners.

IX

Refuge in Heroics

In the cosy activities of this absorbing parish life the war seemed to recede into the distance. We had no close relatives involved in it, nor even our closest friends in the parish, since many had vital jobs in the pit. It might have completely lost its reality for me had it not been for my parents' tremendous anxiety about the course it took and their longing for up-to-date news.

In those days when there was no wireless or television – there was not even a telephone in our house – we were entirely dependent on the papers for news. Only the morning one was delivered, so almost every evening, though he was tired after a long day in the parish, my father would get out his old bicycle and cycle often through a bad winter night, to Blythe Bridge two or three miles away. Here there was a paper shop which got the evening edition as soon as the local train came in.

He used to describe how he stood there with an impatient little crowd, and the rush there was to pick the papers up and read them directly they were given out. But greatly to his sorrow he noted that the young miners, who formed a large part of the crowd, did not rush to peruse the headlines about the war on the front page, but turned the paper over to the back in order to see the latest football news. This was a source of great disappointment to him and my mother since they were very caught up in the patriotic enthusiasm of the day. Although they were very concerned about the individual problems of poor families personally, I don't think they ever realised that a group of young men who till recently had been living at poverty level mostly under a kind of industrial dictatorship, might be a little lukewarm at defending the thing. Now so vital to the war effort their wages were spiralling upwards and they were getting the first taste of affluence they had ever known. Was it surprising therefore that they felt the power of it and wanted to gamble on football, a familiar sport to them, in order to get even more.

When my father returned with the papers he used to read them aloud to my mother and discuss the situation. I recall the agonised to and fro-ing of the endless battles which took place in those days. It was like the bulletins of a patient who was critically ill, and never seemed to completely recover, but went on and on in the acute state causing an endless nightmare of anxiety.

Finally one day it was too much for me. The old fear about the Germans coming over here and killing the cats came up most. I burst into tears and sobbed about my terror in my mother's arms. So far as I can recall, enthused by the patriotism of the moment she was able to offer more comfort and determination that we would win and keep the Germans from our shores, than she had done in 1914 in spite of the news of some major defeat our troops had just suffered, which caused my anxiety to overflow. It was then that she turned to my father and said that they must never again mention the war news in front of me, a rule he at once agreed to and one they kept conscientiously in the ensuing years.

After this divorce from reality I became particularly sensitive to the patriotic and idealistic view of war which was the current one at that time and to which even my humane and peace-loving parents subscribed, a strange contradiction to so much that they stood for.

I recall how my father returned from the bank one day in a state of mixed indignation and distress because of what was considered the extraordinary sentiments expressed by a very close clergyman friend of ours whom he met in there.

'Old Payne had better be careful he does not get locked up,' my father exclaimed on his return to my mother. 'Do you know what he said in the bank? He said that some of the Germans were wonderful people.'

'Oh, he didn't, Daddy!' my mother exclaimed and I remember noticing how strangely hurt and distressed she looked, almost as if she had received a physical injury. I suppose it was hard for her to assimilate what seemed to them at that time something near traitorism with the personal regard she had for an old friend and neighbour.

It did not seem to strike them as strange in those days that they, as representatives of a doctrine that preached universal brotherhood and love for one's enemies, should feel it an obligation to condemn all the people of a particular nation out of hand. Nurse Cavell had not yet spoken her last words to a war-mad world:

'Patriotism is not enough. I must have no hatred or bitterness towards anyone.'

We little knew then that when the next war came we should be in the fore-front of the Peace Movement.

I recall that our clerical friend's utterance alarmed me at first because it reduced my present delight in the heroic, but then I recalled that he was the friend who always alluded to the zeppelins as the Zee-pelins for some reason, I felt he was definitely an oddity, not to be taken much notice of, and went back thankfully to the majority opinion of the nobility of war.

Undoubtedly my enthusiasm for this was richly fed on the kind of books I was reading at that time. So many stories reflected this point of view at that time. But my great enthusiasm for sailors which I had had all my life, strangely, although I had met few, made me especially attracted to a book my brother had entitled, *The Heroic Deeds of the British Navy*. This became like a bible to me. I read every story again and again and worshipped the heroes in it. I still recall the cold chill I felt when, on showing a picture of the *Bluecher* turning turtle, some grown-up pointed out that the black dots running over its side were really human men and that although they were our enemies they were not necessarily all brutes, and needed our compassion.

I can recall even now how this pierced my armour and threatened to undermine some driving force in my life. It was like taking the carburetter out of a car, nothing worked without it. I hastily thrust the idea out of my mind and went back to more hero stories.

Occasionally events in the war impinged on our peaceful life. I recall one especially because it related to my idol, the British Navy. When we were bicycling to see my brother at his prep school, and, as we passed through our home country where we knew people, we became aware that there had been a major naval engagement. In those days when there was no wireless, news travelled in what would seem to us a strangely primitive way, by word of mouth if the papers were not just delivered. I can recall the scraps of information that flew back at me as my mother slowed down to ask people we met coming back from the station and such place of communication, for details of it all, till we pinned it together mentally like a jigsaw puzzle.

This was the Battle of Jutland, hailed then as a great victory for the British Navy, but now merely an historical event the results of which are in the realms of controversy. The reality of it was tremendously brought home to us when we arrived at my brother's school and found that one of the boys who had actually been at school with him there had gone down as a young midshipman on one of the battleships. I recall that my mother was deeply shocked by this, for he was only about fourteen years old and she could identify herself so well with the midshipman's mother, having a son of her own. Her mother love came first in spite of her apparent terrific patriotism. On the whole, our day was overcast with gloom, but I was able to compensate for this by my elation over the glories of the British Navy fighting manfully, and could not see why the grown-ups could not do the same.

Only on one other occasion I think did the war actually impinge at all on our own life personally, and through an unexpected source.

One of the great drawbacks of Nanny having left us was that when I went to bed at night I had to be alone upstairs until my parents came at a much later hour. This was a great change for me after always having the companionship of my brother and Nanny and even being sung to sleep by her. My special dread was that my mother would leave the house altogether. I should not be able to call her up from downstairs if I woke and felt lonely. She therefore gave me a solemn promise that she would never go outside the door once I had gone to bed. On the whole my mother was very good at keeping to her word once given to us children, a fact which established great trust and confidence between herself and her children.

I therefore felt most indignant when I awoke to the sound of several terrific thumps which I immediately identified as resulting from my mother banging the back door mat against the side of the house to shake the dust out. I called lustily and my mother came at once to see what was the matter.

When I explained, she laughed heartily, declaring she had never been outside the door at all and as she pointed out, she would hardly be banging the door mat clean on a cold winter night out in the dark. She explained that Daddy had just come in after a tiring bicycle ride to fetch the papers and had opened a bottle of whisky to have a glass with dinner. The corkscrew had made a rather strange sound. She thought it must be that. I was convinced it was not, and so I went off to sleep and she back to the kitchen, both declaring one another's explanation as wrong.

We did not learn the cause of the noise till next morning, when, strangely enough just as after Jutland, we were setting off on a bicycle trip somewhere. The first person we met was an old man called Gilbert who worked as a local gardener. He was coming up the road slowly on his way to work, but so overwhelmed was he by the news that he must have compelled my mother to get off her bike to hear it.

Did we know he said that a zeppelin had actually got as far as Fenton Collieries last night and tried to drop bombs on it? Luckily these had missed their target and fallen on to some waste land and one even went into a pond there. So no one was hurt.

My mother expressed great relief at this news, and hurried on gathering more scraps of news about the episode as we passed people we knew.

This then was the explanation of the bumps I had heard. I do not recall that I was the least alarmed by this news, in fact I think I was relieved that my mother really had kept her promise and was not banging mats outside the back door. The visitation of this giant meant nothing to me.

When some years later I was out for a quiet country walk in the secure days of peace, and I suddenly saw the ill-fated *R 101* emerge from the screen of tall trees and sail inevitably across the immediate sky, I realised something of the terror such giants, out of all proportion to the usual objects before one's vision, could create. It was a good thing that one had not presented itself to my visual faculties that night, or the bangs would not have remained a confused memory to laugh at, accounted for by doormats.

I suppose however that war-time strains and bad food did begin to tell on our health ultimately, for in 1917 my brother came home for the Christmas holidays with a particularly bad type of flu. He developed an abcess in the ear, and was for a time delirious. It was when he was in this latter acute state that he called my mother urgently and addressed her as 'Clumpy'. Why he thought of this word we never knew, but it stuck in some strange way and became his pet name for her for the rest of his life.

When my brother began to get better my mother became very worried about me. I recall the doctor being asked to look at me in the nursery as he left Ralph's bedside. He listened to my heart and pronounced me as perfectly well, however. I was puzzled at her anxiety as I did not seem to have any of the usual symptoms of a sore throat or cold, or even any shivers though I think I felt a bit off colour. Whether my mother had a premonition or whether her motherly anxiety surrounded me with the wrong thoughts and encouraged the germs to develop I don't know, but by next day I was strangely ill, with a kind of ill feeling I had never felt before. I remember the day after when my brother, who seemed surprisingly to have noticed the fact that I was ill, called through from the other nursery 'How are you?' when I first awoke, I said, 'Oh, better than yesterday.' But I knew I was not so really. It was as if I had receded in a strange way from the active contact and feverish restlessness of this world which I had passed through yesterday. Now everything seemed remote and strange as if seen through a curtain which muffled things. 'As through a glass darkly,' but I did not get as far as the second part of the text – 'then face to face', for I struggled against the illness and returned to normal life again. I cannot say that I found at that age nearly dying was the pleasant experience some people feel it to be. This was probably because I feared anything that would take me away from my home and my parents to which I clung so tenaciously, and the undermining of my physical forces by this exhausting illness – it was diagnosed as pneumonia – was not replaced by any joy through being in contact with another level of existence which must have been just round the corner really.

The whole experience seemed, on looking back, to be associated with the lines of that hymn we used to sing on those cosy Sunday evenings round the piano –

'Peace, perfect peace, death shadowing us and ours.'
But the additional line – 'Jesus has vanquished death and all its powers,' had no saving reality for me. In fact I could never sing that hymn afterwards on a Sunday evening without a shudder.

Of course in those days pneumonia had to work through to the crisis as there were no antibiotics to hasten its termination. But somehow I came to this and turned the right corner, withdrew from the realms of limbo and returned tenaciously to this earthly sphere again.

We were lucky in having a marvellous spell of frost and sunny weather that year after Christmas, and the Hall Pool, as it was known – a kind of lake that belonged to our Squire, froze deeply enough for skating. It was the rarest thing to get such prolonged winter sunshine in our northern clime as we got then. The dazzling sparkle of the snow and ice around us enraptured me. This new form of locomotion on skates, though alarming, gave me a tremendous thrill. A path was swept through the snow round the edge of the pool so that the grown-ups could tour round sedately in an ordered pattern. I liked to follow my own course off the beaten track through the snow glistening, untouched by the foot of man. And if I did fall the experience was cushioned both physically and psychologically by this dazzling white mass into which I was precipitated.

This pleasant occupation was interrupted all too soon however by the return of bad weather, and also by the suggestion from Granny that we should visit her at Bournemouth where she always wintered with my Aunt Nellie – in order to give me a change away after my illness. Such a suggestion coming from Granny was almost in the nature of a royal command and we accepted right away.

X

Convalescence at Bournemouth

We went to Bournemouth a week later to join my grandmother on her winter sojourn there. She and my mother's sister, Aunt Nellie who was unmarried, always installed themselves in a suite of rooms overlooking the sea for the winter. In those days, the lack of servants having made it impossible to live in their old home, the life of the older generation was carefully and elaborately planned, and even a world war seemed to disintegrate it very little.

I remember the night we arrived. We had pork with the cracknell on it for dinner. I had never had it before. It was served in the bow window of Granny's big sitting-room facing the sea, which was impressively draped by heavy curtains. We were told that we must not draw them back to look out on account of the danger of submarines seeing the light from the coast. That is the only time I recall any mention of a black-out in the first world war.

When we descended to the beach the next day, we found this precaution was only too justified. The place was black with people, picking up boxes of matches from a Swedish ship, which had been torpedoed during the night.

We stayed at Bournemouth for some weeks. It was supposed to be a nice change for us, but actually the need for adjustment between our differing ways of life was such as to make it anything but a rest cure. My Aunt was very difficult, especially with my mother, the supposed ugly duckling, who had, much to the family's surprise, married and turned out the swan. I came to understand afterwards how much my aunt was the victim of the pointless aridity of 'Life with Mother', practised in those days.

When, in her extreme old age, she blossomed out as an honorary worker for a political party and became far easier to get on with and far better in health, I realised how much had been pent up in her, and how different she might have been if she had lived in an age when girls were expected to have a career. The early blue stockings were only just beginning to fight their way through opposition to the idea at the time when she was young. As Aunt Nellie was so handsome and had many admirers, marriage was considered to be her obvious 'career'. But few if any of them ever got as far as asking her to share their life permanently because she did not resemble the formal romantic image they had been brought up to think of for a wife.

The first thing my aunt did was to announce that there was an epidemic of black measles in the town, and that my mother must not go to church. You could go to the cinema, she said, because they took the roof off the one at Alum Chine, and let the fresh air in at half time, an early form of air conditioning, but not church. My mother, who had grown rather devout since she married, was very distressed by this, but kept quiet for fear of giving offence. As well as such events of direct opposition, the whole tempo of our lives was strained.

It seemed strange after the rushed life of the Vicarage and our preoccupation with the problems of others, to be in an environment where people sat about and discussed such matters as the relative standards of service in different hotels, and of course the quality of the meals was a very important matter, too. I also recall hearing them discussing whether the drawers of the bedroom furniture glided in and out more easily in the Pump Room Hotel at Bath or the Bath Hotel at Bournemouth. This seemed a sufficiently important factor to influence the final decision as to which place they should go to for the next winter.

My aunt and grandmother's attitude to social contacts was quite different to ours. All and sundry came to the vicarage whenever they liked. My grandmother limited her contacts with the outside world to carefully chosen friends who called at specially appointed times. To have too many friends was considered by them to be foolish, even dangerous, and held to be some sort of disgrace almost akin to moral promiscuity, a sin they suspected us of committing.

My grandmother was a rather handsome old lady. She had

a beautiful fresh complexion, and lovely white hair that rippled back from her forehead up to the pile of coils on the top of her head. She wore striking pale grey suits with rolled lapels decorated with braid. These, and her blouses which were boned and shaped, were all made to measure by a famous Bournemouth dressmaker of that time. The blouses were made of rather stiff, printed silk, and were always in shades of grey and mauve, with shadowy rose and lilac patterns on them. She wore bonnets, of course, as was the fashion for old ladies in those days. These had a kind of raised tulle front, with delicious little flower gardens nestling inside. She had a charming speaking voice, and had sung quite a lot in her youth in Victorian drawing-rooms after dinner. But my grandfather, a hard hunting man who had no taste for such things, had caused her to drop it after her marriage through his scathing criticism of her performances. She had a good sense of humour, in spite of the difficulties she had encountered, but like everything else in her life, it was orderly and confined to certain limits. She scarcely ever laughed with us children, so far as I can recall. She did not approve of our happy-go-lucky upbringing, and so we went terribly in awe of her, for fear we should inadvertently do something she did not approve of.

When we walked across the public gardens to see the shops, as we did most mornings, in brilliant winter sunshine so exciting and unbelievable after the bleak northern winter from which we came, I was not able to skip happily about as the morning called for, but had to walk sedately beside Granny at a leisurely, dignified pace. I was very shy, and became irritated with my grandmother for wanting me by her side. In those days I understood nothing about the pride grandmothers take in their grandchildren, and their wish to get to know them and see them looking at their best, on state visits of this kind. Part of this process of pleasing Granny was a visit to the hairdresser's, at her expense, in order to improve the appearance of my hair, I suppose. I found this episode, of having my hair drastically cut and singed, irritating, and even frightening. I remember the hairdresser gave my mother a booklet in which she tactfully indicated there were some pages on the care of children's hair. I felt this was an inference that she thought my mother had neglected mine and I felt very offended.

Having furbished me up, Granny took seats for *Peter Pan*. I was rather surprised that my mother was not also invited, so used was I to going about as a family party. I did not realise that it was all part of this proprietorship in grandchildren that she wanted to have me on my own. We sat in one of the front rows of the stalls, and what impressed me most – for even in those days I was interested in the supernatural – was the way Peter Pan levitated and flew round the stage. It seemed an entrancing mystery. So far as I remember, the wires were quite invisible to me.

A few days later, an old friend of Granny's who was evidently also infected by this desire of the aged to enjoy the entertainment of the young – invited me out to tea at the Bath Hotel. This rather offended Granny and Aunt Nellie – they felt it was usurping their protégée, but they agreed that I must accept.

This lady, however, had lately undergone a somewhat extensive internal operation quite common to women today, but in those days rather an innovation, and my grandmother and aunt seemed to think it might have dangerous results mentally. I remember them solemnly warning me that I was to keep very quiet whilst I was out with this lady, as she might get up and shout and wave her arms about, or do almost anything. Needless to say, having a child's curious mind, I was rather intrigued by this possibility. But I did as I was told, and kept very quiet during the outing, awaiting developments.

We had a very pleasant time together, and I was initiated into the glories and sparkle of a Bath Hotel tea. And what a splendid meal tea was in those days, such a cosy glamour against the background of a string orchestra playing sentimental tea time music with a room full of elegantly dressed ladies gossiping.

My hostess, a solid, middle-aged lady, the daughter of a famous Leicester woollen manufacturer, appeared to behave quite normally and was much more friendly and easy to get on with than my grandmother. When I returned to our rooms and had nothing abnormal to report, I felt she and Aunt were most disappointed.

In those days, Bournemouth was a place of considerable social elegance, its population was residential rather than holiday-making. Even visitors came for long periods, and brought an entourage of servants and nannies for the children and large quantities of luggage. Besides this there were all the old people and the invalids who went about in huge bath chairs drawn by attentive servants or hired ones firmly at the pier. This slow, solemn disintegration of the physical was very depressing.

The road to the Bath Hotel was so quiet in those days that I thought it was a private one. The clients who sailed dignifiedly out of its impressive doorway, or into the Crystal Palace-like labyrinth of the Winter Garden, were primarily retired colonels and their wives, of a high social status. Sir Dan Godfrey had by then succeeded in his fight to establish the high reputation for a municipal orchestra, and a crowd of people, fashionable rather than deeply musical, thronged the Winter Garden at all musical programmes. In fact, it became almost a social obligation to go.

But the social obligations and limitations of life at Bournemouth were not an ideal setting either for my mother or myself. One or other of us were always 'putting our foot in it', and so it was with some relief that we said goodbye when our time to return home came at last. I had learnt much of the things that divided our two worlds, occupied by my mother's family, and that of my father's. We were both glad, I think, to exchange this opulence and comfort for the happy-go-lucky life in our shabby vicarage. We were not meant for 'the Establishment'.

XI

Visits to Nanny's Home

In the spring Ralph came home from school with measles and I was sent away to Nanny's to avoid infection. I stayed there six weeks, which was long enough to make me feel really part of that environment.

I have always been glad that I had this opportunity to experience life at the level of the ordinary person in the village community. At the Vicarage we listened to many complaints from the cottagers about their difficulties and did our best to intervene on their behalf with the powers that be. In our own home, however, we were reasonably free to do what we liked within the limits of our modest income. The ruling of the Ecclesiastical Commissioners was only operative in some major problems. I had no idea, therefore, till I went to stay at Nanny's how frustrating it could be if one's domestic arrangements were subject to the dictates of a terse and evasive agent acting on behalf of some remote titled personage with whom you could never have any contact to explain the individual urgencies and details of your problem.

At Nanny's I got to know the life of the village children too, for I played freely with them out in the road, a thing I was never allowed to do even in our democratic vicarage. It was just not done in those days; even my mother in spite of her readiness to scrub her own doorstep accepted this taboo. Always so zealous for our welfare, and so careless of her own, I think she feared that we should catch some infectious disease, or a local accent, either of which might have been damaging to our careers.

There were the Whittington children who lived at the farm across the road but I still remember Lottie Riley, a little girl who lived up the hill, best because of a rather spectacular event connected with her. One day she quite unaccountably stuffed Indian corn, intended for the chickens, up her nose. Why she engaged in this extraordinary occupation I don't think anyone stayed to find out owing to the panic that ensued. It was an indication of Nanny's great reputation for dealing with children that Lottie's mother rushed her down to Nanny's cottage as the first source of help. I am glad to say Nanny's resourcefulness was equal to the occasion. She seized up Nanniemigger's button hook she usually used for her boots and after some screams and protestations on Lottie's part succeeded in fishing the offending objects out of her nose like raking ashes out of the back of the grate. There was much applause for this from the women now involved in the emergency and Lottie was marched off home with severe admonishments from her mother never to do that again.

Nanny's house was a typical Shropshire home. It was called Hurst Cottage and situated near the village of Wheeton Aston. It was very cosy in comparison to the majority of houses in our village in a more northern clime. Built in a sheltered position in a valley, it was surrounded by a mature and abundant cottage garden which seemed to have grown up naturally like flowers over the sloping ground.

Most of our time was spent in the sitting room on the right hand side of the front door. It had a personality of its own. It had never been invaded, thank goodness, by the hideous monotony of the mass-produced suite on the H.P. Nanny's father had been the village carpenter and most of the furniture being hand-made by him, was the work of a craftsman. In fact each article in the room was an individual about which Nanny could give some interesting history, from the kitchen cupboard (made by her father) on whose doors she used to check my growing height, to the exquisitely lovely 'off white' tea cups of old porcelain with antique gold spots that had belonged to her grandmother.

Nanniemigger, as we always called Nanny's mother, derived from a childish attempt of my brother's to pronounce her name when he was very young, always sat in her own special chair by the fire. This was not a hard ladder-backed one like the old people used on the moorland farms at home, but something less austere, and more in keeping with the quiet relaxed atmosphere of this pastoral land. It was a rocking chair with an oak frame decoratively twisted and a wide band of cream tapestry stitched across to form the seat and back.

It appealed to me like the rocking horse at home. I loved to be allowed to sit in it and go to and fro as far as Nanniemigger's anxiety for her indispensable possession would permit.

When we arrived tea was always ready, laid on a shining white cloth with crisp lettuce from the garden and watercress from a local bed. To eat with this there was bread and butter beautifully cut by Nanny's practised hand.

There were boiled eggs in cream earthenware cups with cocks on them. The eggs at Nanny's were always deep brown and tasted particularly good because they were laid by Nanny's own hens with whom I came to have a personal acquaintance. She kept six Rhode Island Reds in the disused pigsty up the garden. One of them, the palest of the group, who went by the name of Rhoda, was a most obliging creature. If invited into the house she would be perfectly happy to play the part of mannequin, in Ivy, the doll's, green cape. She would strut across the floor importantly, a perfectly possessed model, but flirting here and there with her beak at any interesting tit-bit she might encounter in a momentary lapse into her natural role in life.

There was only one chilly, alarming spot in the house; to this we repaired to wash up after tea. That was the back kitchen, on the left of the front door. The dark brick floor, the primitive walls, from which the whitewash seemed to be always falling in spite of Nanny's care of things, filled me with a terrifying chill. Even the sandstone sink seemed to be more damp and musty than the usual ones were. The whole atmosphere appeared to me to find its central focus in an old Victorian coloured print, framed in a deep, slightly inward-sloping frame of reddish brown wood like mahogany. Perhaps that was what made it seem so real. The picture was one of the ruins of Whitby Abbey.

When I first arrived, feeling a little home-sick and insecure, even at Nanny's, I used to gaze at this picture apprehensively. The stark ruins against the sunset sky and the glimpse of the cold grey sea just beyond seemed full of decay and gloom and both fascinated and repelled me. It made me think of that sorrow in the world I was always trying to ignore. I was not to know then what a whole new vista of happiness lay waiting for me across that cold northern sea, and with what different feelings I should come to regard it when I crossed it on my many journeys to Norway.

The garden was a joy to a child, full of little paths, one could run along, stone steps and rose arches. Nanny knew all the plants well by name and as individuals. She never bought any en masse from a nurseryman, but acquired them by the painstaking efforts of a personal collector getting a root from one friend here or a cutting from which to root a plant from another. They all flourished because of the love and care she gave them.

Of course, there was a lot to do in the garden and I recall one red-letter day when Nanny had a helper – a young man called Henry Poles. He was a very kind, genuine person who had been chauffeur at a neighbouring rectory when Tippo was cook. But he had been inevitably 'swept up' into the vast Army we had on the French front at that time and was wearing khaki instead of a chauffeur's uniform. He had brass letters on the shoulder of his tunic. They were K.S.L.T. which I thought looked rather fine. Nanny explained that they stood for King's Shropshire Light Infantry. As it belonged to the King it seemed to me something to be rather proud of.

Henry soon shed his tunic to undertake some hard work. When he rolled up his sleeves he showed us his arm which had some ugly marks on it. He explained that that was where some shrapnel had gone into it and there were some pieces the doctor could not get out so they would have to leave them there, a fact Nanny showed great sympathy about.

It was a glorious day of moving plants to new corners of the garden, straightening up the rockery and all sorts of things. I followed it all with great interest and felt Henry was a splendid new friend. Like my mother, I delighted in getting things done. He never showed any impatience in my wish to participate in these activities and even played with me at times. The day went all too fast and Henry said farewell to us and departed to his home and ultimately to France.

A week or so later Nanny opened a letter while I was having

breakfast. I can see her now. Suddenly she burst into tears. This was very surprising to me because I don't think I had ever seen Nanny cry before. It was we who cried usually and ran to Nanny for comfort. Presently, when she could speak, she told us that Tippo had written to say that Henry had been killed in France a few days after his return there. He was of course one of thousands of similar young men who were being killed every week, but it was only this personal touch that brought this grim fact home to me.

In spite of this loss I do not recall that it disturbed for me the wonderful peace surrounding Nanny's home. When I was in the garden alone I liked to go up to the gap in the hedge by the hen run, where someone had felled a tree, and gaze out over the rich pastures, feel the warm air heavy with the scent of hay or wild flowers pouring in on me. Then I would listen to the hens' contented pratings, rising to a crescendo at times as they reiterated their acceptance of the goodness of life. It has always seemed ever since that this was the embodiment of the peace and abundance of an English summer's day.

We often took expeditions to see Nanny's friends and I have retained in my mind like a vivid dream the day Nanny and I visited the Bent Farm, as it was curiously named. We had crossed one or two of the rich fields one overlooked from Nanny's garden when we came to the last fence. It was a huge stile, but somehow I got over it first and literally tumbled down into the orchard on the other side. When I picked myself up and looked around it seemed to me as if we had entered the Elysian fields. Lady's smocks, cowslips and wild flowers galore peopled the extremely bright green grass spread out under the apple trees.

I bent down hastily to gather some for fear they faded away for the smoke from the coal pits and the cold climate limited our wild flowers so much they seemed unreal. Cowslips have always been a special delight to me, perhaps because of their affinity of colour with the buttercup, but also because the first time I ever saw them was growing in abundance in the grass around me on that memorable summer day.

The next year we *all* decided to go and stay with Nanny for our holiday, which was a great event. To get there we hired an old-fashioned coach, or perhaps one would call it a brake. It belonged to Lymer, who was our local hire man. It was a vehicle with a bench seat running right round it against the wall. It required two horses to draw it.

I was put inside with some beagles and not only the family luggage, but also a lot of food that Mummy took to help with our keep. I remember for instance that soon after we started off at a triumphant trot one of the beagles got excited, trying to jump on and off the seats to see out of the window and put her foot through a paper top into a jam pot. No one worried very much. We had little knowledge of microbes in those days – the chief fear in the nursery was infectious diseases like scarlet fever.

The brake had a low door at the back, over which I could look out and keep an eye on my parents and Ralph who formed an exuberant cavalcade behind.

It must have been about thirty miles to Nanny's but at last we arrived and somehow packed into her little cottage. I seem to recall that I had a bed in the same front bedroom and shared it with my father and mother this time.

We must have been lucky in having good weather that summer or perhaps I have an Elysian memory of the days spent there – on no other holidays do I remember coming in touch so much with the 'grass roots'. The joyous warmth of an August day, the warm scents which accumulated in uncultivated corners where the hedges were thick with late flowering wild flowers and baking dry grass when the ground had been left unmown.

All this seemed to link with the solidity of historical monuments we visited in the neighbourhood, stone ruins baking in the sun. I specially recall a visit to Tong Castle, since pulled down, for although it was, I think, something of a pseudo-antique its towering walls impressed me greatly.

I recall that on the way there down a lane I committed a terrible entomological faux pas. There in the cosy warmth of grass beside the footway I glimpsed a rare sight, a huge Leopard moth. Knowing how Ralph coveted such a valuable specimen for his collection which we had so often seen in the moth book I turned a deaf ear to his frenzied appeals to wait. I suppose I wanted to be the first to gather it and then present it to him, also I was afraid it would run away. Excitedly I rushed forward and flung my sun bonnet over it. It was only when this deed was done that Ralph was able to explain that we had just come on it as it had emerged from the chrysalis and it needed vital time to 'spread'. Whether I had irretrievably damaged it I can't recall. I seem to remember that we did not have it in our collection so perhaps we left it to go on 'spreading'.

The most memorable expedition, however, was to Boscobel because it was famous for events in the King Charles period to which I had felt so strongly linked and about which I had written my first book.

There was the great oak tree where Charles actually went to sleep when in hiding and snored a little, and the story of how the Roundheads came there searching for him but decided there could be no-one there because a pigeon flew out of the tree. Presumably, the pigeon had been unaware of the sleeping king.

Then there was the quaint little wooden summer house like an upturned boat on a mound, which was said to contain the underground escape tunnel and the garden where he 'spent the day reading in a pretty arbour', strange artistic appreciation in such a time of stress. The house kindly and beautiful, with leaded panes in windows looking out on to the garden. There was the priests' hiding hole which ran down the house on the inside wall at the back of the room. This was the first I had ever seen.

There were pictures of the faithful Penderels, the Catholic woodcutters who sheltered him and on the picturesque top floor an attic room with a spinning wheel which especially delighted me. Going back to see the house in more recent years I missed this appropriate relic of the industrious Penderel family and asked where it had gone. The guide had no knowledge of it. When she asked how long ago it was that I saw it I counted up and realised it was forty years, which caused her to display some justified impatience at my inquiry.

I have been to Boscobel many times since and it seems to have remained strangely undisturbed in modern times, a kind of crucible for the history of that period.

During that stay at Nanny's I learnt so much of history in a way that suited my appetite far more than the exact text books which filled my mind at school with dead facts. Although I was only a small child I have never forgotten what I heard and saw there.

We returned to Dilhorne in September and then the autumn having passed we were plunged into the rigours of winter in that big cold house which it was now very difficult to heat on account of high prices and lack of fuel in the war. The cheerful glow of the nursery fire had been replaced by a tall oil stove which displayed a static pattern of light on the ceiling rather like a perforated paper mat, the lid being made in this way to allow the heat to rise from the wick below.

Ralph brought home the 'flu again from school and history almost repeated itself. I developed it just at Christmas again and the doctor had to be called on that day because I had a high temperature. My mother was so worried about me, thinking I was getting pneumonia again that she swallowed a large piece of her dental plate with the Christmas turkey. Unfortunately, it had a hook on it, so she began to worry about herself also for fear she got ill and could not look after me. However, the family doctor arrived and reassured the family as he did in those days, by saying that I had not got pneumonia, but only bronchitis and there was no need to worry about the piece of plate with the hook on it because he had swallowed exactly the same part of his own plate years ago and never felt any ill effects at all.

I think I quite enjoyed that illness, because I did not feel really ill as I had done the year before, and it seemed rather comfortable to rest in bed as the centre of interest and attention. It gave me such a sense of security.

In spite of my inactivity, however, I recall achieving one piece of personal development. I had become very keen on cross stitch, because of the lovely old samplers that Nanny had and her own use of the stitch in embroidering needlebooks, etc. Someone had given me a piece of canvas divided into large squares on which I intended to embroider the whole alphabet. I recall one morning, when feeling better, I felt the time had come to start on this momentous task. I asked my mother to draw an A for me, but she said I must wait till she had done something urgent downstairs and she would return presently. She emphasized, as was the custom of those days when children were not encouraged to be independent, that of course I could not do it myself, I must wait for her to lay the foundation stone so to speak. When she did not return for what seemed an interminably long time I felt challenged and irritated and had actually drawn one and done it myself. I still recall when my mother came upstairs and saw it how superior I felt and almost condescending at her apologies for delay and admiration of my attainment. I still have the canvas, and what vibrations of personal achievement that A of woolly pink gives off. I regret to say that the rest of the alphabet was only filled in here and there for the whole task was never finished, but the A was a landmark in my life.

The spring brought bad news of the war; we seemed to be losing ground in that endless battle which had now gone on for what seemed such an interminable time for that one small area of France and Belgium which formed the battlefield of the first world war.

At Easter came Haig's famous speech about our backs to the wall. I recall that my father who did not often express his patriotic views loudly was moved to deliver a special sermon in which he excitedly challenged the congregation to defeat the enemy. We were much impressed by this, but actually taken outside its parochial category it could not have had a very great effect on anyone. The last members of our village who were of any active age had already been conscripted. I do not remember being very disturbed by this, I had long ago become so indoctrinated by the patriotic idea I was reckless about our safety and I could not admit defeat.

I do not recall that we indulged in a holiday at all that summer, perhaps that was why in the autumn I was sent away to stay with Nanny again. It was a wonderful time for walking and Nanny had such a long experience of the country there and knowledge of lanes we could wander down, which meandered in between thick hedges always beckoning us on to the next bend lest there should be something exciting round the corner.

We often met the local pigs setting forth on similar expeditions in small groups, for it was the custom at that time of year to turn them loose to eat acorns, probably a very valuable and natural addition to their diet.

Later on in the season, however, I became conscious that a strange melancholy had crept into the sighing of the wind, especially in the ash trees – more than in the hardy oak. There seemed to be something ominous about their sound. It pursued me down local lanes mysteriously. I tried in vain to escape from it, feeling it was linked with the inevitable tragedies of this earthly life which I was always seeking to ignore.

It was during this autumn visit to Nanny that I recall lying lazily in the comfort of my bed upstairs and listening to the activities of preparations for breakfast down below. There was the brisk raking of the grate to clear it fully of ashes, and the pleasant jink of teaspoons being set out quickly on saucers. From the peace of this familiar rhythm I was suddenly aroused by the voice of the postman speaking in an unusually high-pitched and excited way. He was evidently imparting some news of importance. He spoke as one who has inside information and is a little proud of it.

'They say as we are going to have one of these – er – armersticks,' he shouted, thinking others were deaf like himself.

'What is an armerstick?' I asked myself lazily, lying up there in the warmth and comfort. It did not appear to be anything I was wanting to acquire so I decided not to worry about it but to turn over and doze off again.

When I finally descended to breakfast Nanny was laughing over the episode.

'Funny old man,' she was saying, 'fancy pronouncing a word like "armistice" like that.'

'But, Nanny,' I asked, 'What is an armistice?'

'It is what you have at the end of a war,' she explained. 'He means the war may be coming to an end.'

I do not recall being particularly amazed or elated at this news, and having solved the problem of the meaning of the word armistice seemed to dismiss it from my mind. I had by now become so indoctrinated with the patriotic ethic and steeped myself in *The Heroic Deeds of the British Navy* – to which I had now added *A Tall Ship* and *Naval Occasions* by Bartimeus that possibly I was not at all keen to see its termination. The truth was, I think, that I had managed to contract out of the

(a) The back drive. The sycamore tree up which I used to climb and watch he outside world is in the background.

(b) Ralph and I with Lofty, the beagle who occupied the stall at choir practice.

'Ma', born in a rabbit hole, and a[
said to be looking apprehensively f[
the Germans.

'Her Lenten Fast'. The three cats from left to right are Mr Pym, Lady Gray and
Ma, and the beagle is Lofty.

reality of war. The possibility of the Germans reaching our cosy island seemed quite remote now. Even Haig's famous 'backs to the wall' speech which my father had commented on at Easter in his sermon, had failed to fill me with any sense of real danger, only with patriotic fervour.

After I came back home from Nanny's that Autumn my mother and I set out rather early on some shopping expedition to Blythe Bridge, a few miles away. We must have completed it rather soon for before eleven o'clock we started on our way home. I was riding as usual on the carrier at the back of my mother's bike.

Half way home we came to a steep hill and my mother dismounted and lifted me down. We walked up the hill in a leisurely fashion. It must have been quite mild for the time of year for there seemed no urge to hurry to keep warm. It was one of those late autumn days on which a strange stillness hung over everything. As I followed my mother's measured footsteps up the hill there was nothing to indicate that we were treading into a new era of history.

We reached the top at last and paused for a moment to rest and look back at the valley. Then, suddenly, a strangely sharp sound rent the air. It was the hooter at a colliery over towards the Potteries in the direction from which we had come. It seemed a shrill and crude disturber of the peaceful air. And then we heard our local colliery take up the strain, and another and another, as the volume grew and spread like some vast patchwork of sound over the whole valley as each centre of industry echoed the news.

I remember I stood there amazed, and looked at my mother questioningly and she replied,

'Fancy, Ruth, the war must be over at last.'

And then the great volume of sound gradually died away and we stood looking at the vista below us without speaking. Little did we realise then how this historic moment of silence at 11 o'clock on November 11th 1918 would go echoing down the century, commemorated by kings and queens, battalions of serving soldiers and Old Contemptibles as each anniversary came.

Many years later this solemn silence was broken at the Cenotaph by a man's voice crying, 'War is wrong. Stop war!'

It was indicative of the mental sickness of society that an ambulance was called and he was rushed off at once to a mental hospital and certified as insane.

The world had to go through another period of destruction and slaughter, and then come to the brink of world suicide by the atom bomb, before even a minority could come to realise the truth of this lone voice crying in the wilderness of the world's madness.

XII

Widening Horizons

Neither my brother nor I were caught up in the chaos and disillusion of the early twenties. We were still of school age, where our conventional pattern of life was little disturbed. We did not sing, like the young people in *Cavalcade*, 'What is there to strive for, love or keep alive for, Twentieth Century blues are getting me down'; all that passed us by. I don't even remember being agitated about 'Homes for Heroes', though heroes, especially sailor ones, were still very much in my thoughts. So far as I can recall, our village did not produce any dazzling specimen of emancipated womanhood to bring that current problem before my eyes either.

The most major event in our lives at this time was moving from the big Vicarage into a much smaller one. My mother had become terribly worn out trying to run the old home, which was gradually becoming increasingly shabby, and was far beyond our means to repair. We were very lucky in getting an offer of £1,100 for it. This was considered an enormous sum in those days, and the ecclesiastical authorities responsible consented to accept it, much to our relief.

I do not recall that leaving the house was any great emotional strain to my brother and me, curiously enough, much as we had loved it. I think my mother was the one who felt it most, because her early married life and our childhood days were so linked with that home. These were years in her life which she had loved in spite of the hard work entailed and she knew they would not come again.

We had some very good neighbours next door. I was about the same age as their daughter Marjorie, who became a great friend of mine. The house had been the occasion for many lavish tea parties held in my honour with cream and home made cakes laid on ad lib. It was appropriate therefore, I suppose, that our sojourn at the Old Vicarage, as it now came to be called, should end by hospitality meted out from them.

My mother used to describe how she finally closed the door of the old home very reluctantly, and this kindly neighbour next door invited her in to take a glass of elderberry wine. She was so worn out that the effects of this proved most potent. When a little later she set out to walk to the new house, she was forced to sit down in the hedge when she reached the Church Fields, which were only a little way along the route, and there she burst into tears. Much to her embarrassment, as she sat there, a young parishioner vaulted the nearby stile, looked at her for a moment in astonishment, and then tactfully hurried on as if he had never seen her.

For my brother and I, however, now reaching our teens, there was no looking back but there was the realisation of a wider, unexplored world before us which made us eager for any new experience like this. A new house full of fresh smelling paint and new wallpaper seemed to fit our mood. Ever since that time such smells have carried with them for me a feeling of elation and excited anticipation about opportunities in the future.

The windows wide open on to windswept fields and a distant ridge of woodland on the horizon showed us a wider world than the sheltered lawns of our previous home. It was symbolic I suppose of the new pattern of our lives.

In the new home too I had a room that was really my own, not just an inherited nursery. Even the colour scheme was my own choice. I had the walls covered with an almost aggressive wall paper of huge mauve wistaria hanging in loaded festoons from a mock trellis. I did not realise at the time that through this I had maintained a link with my early memories of the real one on the outside wall of the nursery, and my waking memories of peace and security there. At the new house I never tired of lying in bed and gazing at this almost gaudy replica of nature with its exuberant mauve, turning it over mentally, rather like a juicy sugared sweet.

My father gave me some charming old furniture, a chest of drawers with a deep band of inlay across the top masking two secret drawers which intrigued me. He also bought an old spinet and had it adapted to a smaller size to fit the room. It was a great pity that it had to be altered to give it a functional use. But it still remained a charming piece with a deep ledge at the back beautifully inlaid and the name of the previous owner on it, set in an oval design. Who this was I have never been able to decipher quite but I was very interested when a friend who was a 'sensitive' wrote to me from Cornwall and said, 'I see a spinet in your house and a charming old lady who used to own it often sits at it.' Needless to say, the 'sensitive' had never visited my house at all and seen it.

To a girl entering her teenage there is something very satisfying about having her own dressing table. It is a place where she can sit quietly and regard herself in the mirror and see a new angle as it were of both her physical features and her personality. I remember too with what feelings of delight I seemed to endow the set of blue enamel brushes and the cherished powder bowl my mother had given me.

The garden outside did not hold the mysterious embrasures that our old garden had done. It was merely a piece of level land with a hedge round it enclosing some formal beds for flowers, a vegetable garden, a green field and a cramped little back yard covered with the inevitable blue bricks. My parents put up a shed not far from the back door to make an extra room for us to play in. Outside the window of this I created my own little garden at the end of the vegetable patch. In the centre I put an old sundial we had placed on a sturdy wooden post made out of a tree trunk with a circular grass surround and paths leading off. In the rest of the area I planted those old fashioned flowers – poppies, lupins, love-in-the-mist, etc. – which I had loved so in the old Vicarage garden.

The beds at the front of the house were rather like those at the old Vicarage, clear-cut and formal but the facing was much more sunny and encouraging for plants.

We had a gardener then called Ben Sedgewick, a much valued friend who for some reason was always called 'Potter Boo'. He like my father's Church Warden was one of the winders at the pit and did gardening in his spare time according to what shift he was on.

He had a great liking for calceolarias and wallflowers with an edging of blue lobelias all in exact rows. Certainly the effect was quite striking but I was secretly longing for the disorder of the old garden and more variation in the selection but I never liked to tell him so because he was so proud of the dazzling display his plan produced.

The more confined area of ground set up had an advantage for my brother and me because of the exciting bicycle track it provided with the qualities of an obstacle race. In and out of the small paths we went, though narrow wooden doors into the back yard, bumping wildly over a ridge of bricks that marked the entrance. The doors were set at very odd angles. Through one of them there was literally only half an inch to spare between the cycle and the water butt. To add to the tension and excitement there was always the possibility that we might meet each other in a head-on collision on a blind corner since we always rode in opposite directions and at what seemed to be considerable speed.

At first my mother used to keep popping her head out of the kitchen window in alarm and inveighing against this activity but finally she got used to it and went on quietly with the washing up. I am always glad that she did for I learnt more about how to control a vehicle than I could ever have done through a course of driving lessons. I feel sure this activity and the exciting tobogganning we did in stone wall country helped to make me feel so at home with a car even on modern roads.

Yes, it seemed a good world to us, inside the neat privet hedges of the new Vicarage. My mother was happy in her small 'modern' house. She no longer suffered from fatigue and over-strained nerves as she had done at the old one. My father was less strained too. The war was over so now he had only the duties of his own parish to occupy him. We were indeed lucky. Our family citadel had not in any way been shaken by the tragedies of war, nor by the disillusionment of the post-war world. We did not perceive the strong current of change that was sweeping round us and must ultimately disturb our foundations.

Since for us the old world still hung together, the family believed that the best thing you could do for a boy was to send him to one of the famous public schools. My parents were delighted, therefore, when my grandmother offered to pay my brother's fees. They set out to select the right one out of the many Ralph had been entered for since he was a baby.

Their first choice was Winchester. But this proved over full and expensive. Their second and successful selection was Shrewsbury. This latter school was far more linked with us. My father had held his first curacy at Whitchurch in Shropshire. He still had many friends in the county and loved it dearly. My mother and he used to repair there constantly on bicycles on their precious Mondays off to enjoy not only the company of their friends and also the countryside which meant so much to them. They had spent the first part of their honeymoon in Shrewsbury. It was therefore a place bound to us by ties of long affection.

What the 'new' school out at Kingsland lacked in beauty of structure was compensated for by its exceptional situation. The blue line of the Welsh mountains across the peaceful Shropshire plain on a summer evening after rain had a unique pastoral beauty. How well I came to know it on a Sunday after Evensong in Chapel when we strolled across the vivid green playing fields. On the other side of the school you looked down on to the quarry, with the fringe of great elm trees (now alas! cut down) in the green profusion of high summer and the Severn winding beneath them.

Ralph was lucky in getting a place in a neo-Georgian house that stood a little way from the rest. The Housemaster kept an impeccable bachelor establishment, a drawing room of Louis XV furniture, and a rack in the hall containing 96 walking sticks, one for every time he had crossed over to the Continent, which in those days was quite an achievement.

A whole new world now opened before us. Like the world of Uncle Ernest, it was rather outside our sphere but it was one that appealed to us because it was based on an ideal. We made an effort, therefore, to come to terms with it because it had a meaning for us. Ideologically it was built on the idea of chivalry and self-sacrifice. It was a world in which young men were still taught to take their hats off if they met any member of the school accompanied by a lady, to put women first, not only in doorways but in everything. Last but not least, it taught them to die gloriously for their country.

It was significant and inevitable that the school war memorial should take the shape of a life sized statue of the school's illustrious pupil, Sir Philip Sydney, a shining example of self-sacrifice in war. His last words when he was offered water as he lay dying on the field of Flanders beside another soldier, were carved on its base –

'Thy necessity is yet greater than mine.'

The effigy was aptly chosen. To most parents it was a projection of their own son's action in similar circumstances, to the staff a crystallisation of the spirit the school sought to teach. But none of us asked the salient question, 'Why should the flower of English manhood still be dying in the mud of Flanders hundreds of years after Sir Philip Sydney's brilliant life was sacrificed there?' Our ideals were like sugar round a pill. We swallowed it too eagerly to perceive the real bitterness inside. For one thing the idea of patriotism was too bound up with the religious views we held in those days. We could not come to terms with reality and face the fact of the utter barbarity of war. If we ever felt uncomfortable about it we looked at what then appeared to us the only alternative, the role of traitor and coward.

I turned up a copy of the school magazine *The Salopian* for November 1923 recently. Out of seven poetical contributions three are about death and two are long narrative poems which are entirely occupied with eulogising the fallen of the Great War though it had ended eight years before.

We can smile now at the 'household gods' of that age but what replaced them but the disintegration of society? If only those of us who believed in the ideals of that time so fervently could have transcended them into the greater ideals of international peace, gone to war against the spectre of starvation, which laid the seeds of Nazism, and against the socially destructive forces of the slums. But our ideals were too hothouse. They shrivelled instead of blossoming forth under the chilly winds of new thought in the post-war age.

We could not foresee this so we delighted in the Speech Day Ceremonies and listened with great satisfaction to the school's rendering of the familiar psalm – used each year – 'I was glad when they said unto me we will go into the House of the Lord. Our feet shall stand in thy gates Oh Jerusalem. For Jerusalem is built as a city that is at unity in itself.' But was it really at unity?

Our elevation to the public school sphere posed many difficult economic and social problems at the practical level. First there was the problem of clothes. While our material needs had expanded our income had not. Speech Day had brought that important question 'What should one wear?' very much to the fore for my mother and myself. I still hoped for the more feminine frock, denied me at Christmas parties; my mother still felt a coat and skirt was more practical and insisted on a blue serge one as she said it was useful for so many occasions. We must have been terribly poor for there seemed no prospect of having a thin dress too, to use if the day should be swelteringly hot, as it so often was.

My longing for the feminine, however, was somewhat satisfied by the provision of a specially trimmed hat for the occasion. It was a plain navy blue one to which was added a delicate pleated shell pink lining on the underbrim and a wreath of daisies and forget-me-nots round the crown. It seems a little strange in these days of no hats that with so modest an income my mother afforded a special one for me. On seeing photos of her portrayed in some of the extraordinary creations resembling whole flower gardens that she wore a few years previously I realised one could not appear without one and would hardly undertake the purchase of a hat lightly in those days.

I can still remember the suit my mother wore the first year we went to Speech Day. It was a charming greeny-blue tweed flecked with yellow. This was surmounted by a tricorne hat, in a delicious amber yellow plaited straw which shone and bulged in each twist like a particularly delicious yellow sweet we used to eat called a 'Cushion', so that it actually made my mouth water.

The tricorne was very fashionable in those days and it suited my mother admirably as she was tall and upright with good features and long hair swept up on combs at the front and then back into a bun. I felt very proud of her in this turn-out but of course our poverty had to creep in somewhere and spoil every ensemble. In this case it was her shoes. Apparently, our budget was so strictly limited that she could not possibly afford a 'dressy' pair. She had to wear the usual golf brogues that served her for all parish occasions. I remember these were rather long with a sort of fringed tongue that fell over the instep and covered the lacing. Gillie brogues they were called and rather fashionable in those days for country occasions. But, oh dear, how very out of place they looked among the delicate pointed footwear with bronze buckles and similar decorations that the other mothers wore. I remember my embarrassment when we stepped off the ferry at the boathouse and proceeded up the zig-zag path of cobbles that led to the school. It was the kind of approach that displayed people's shoes so clearly. If you tried to get ahead of the other passengers on the ferry then your feet were even more noticeable as you zig-zagged across their vision just above. There is one bend in that path which is still endowed for me with a feeling of shame and oppression and a visual image of those enormous brogues as my Mother clumped onwards and upwards to the final goal, the wicket gate at the top.

On Speech Day evening it was customary to hold a concert in the school hall. It added a glamour and sparkle to the day when having gone through the marathon of rousing speeches and presentation of prizes in a packed hall on a hot July day, parents returned in the cool of the evening, relaxed and a trifle meditative, sentimentally reflecting on their own school days gone by.

It was appropriate, therefore, that the programme should be rather full of songs with delicate sentiment. The English are not good at such items. They are apt to make them into sentimental songs. But at Shrewsbury they were lucky in having an exceptionally good interpreter among the teaching staff. I do not remember his name. He was a neat, good-looking man with a small moustache and a pleasant smile. His appearance was particularly characteristic of the time. He resembled many young officers just out of the Forces and he had also a certain likeness to Kennerly Rumford, Clara Butt's husband, who was at that time such a popular embellishment to all her recitals.

The corner stone of his repertoire was the Irish song 'The Gentle Maiden'.

I can still hear his clear voice drifting over the hushed expectant school as he sang –

There's one that is pure as an angel,
And fair as the flowers of May,
They call her the Gentle Maiden
Wherever she takes her way.
And whether my prayers be granted
Or whether she pass me by,
The face of that Gentle Maiden
Will follow me till I die.

Such devotion and faith in another human being seems like a fairy tale in these days of stark frankness and shifting matrimonial relationships.

How the audience thrilled to it all and clapped again and again. The older ones because they liked to imagine that they had shared this experience, the younger ones because they were looking forward confidently to having 'Gentle Maidens' of their own. How many found this lasting devotion and unity and how many lost their way in the labyrinth of divorce and disillusionment of the post-war years we cannot know. Life was so different then. The emotions were still so carefully channelled by society into certain directions which were suited to biological needs. It led to humbug and illusion in many cases but for some it nurtured and sheltered a living force within them that blossomed forth under the protection of social custom like a seedling kept under a cloche. It is as refreshing as a whiff of lavender from old clothes now in an age when it is, generally speaking, only the suburban middle class who link romance and economic security together and seem to seek unhesitatingly the married state. While the biggest hit in a leading London musical show runs warningly – 'Oh *never* take a woman in your life.'

My brother at least was never to enter this matrimonial maelstrom since he knew unswervingly his choice from a little boy of eight years old; I feel he would have made that rare thing a happy marriage because Providence had allowed him to meet and recognise his affinity in childhood. But fate had decreed from them separate vocations and their ways of life were to part. This was probably because there was a deep link between them in Eternity, and he did not need the physical unity of an earthly marriage.

I recall that later Ralph bought the score of the 'Gentle Maiden' and used to play it in an evening on our little piano. He had a sensitive touch which made it seem good even on that. In my memory it is all mixed up with *Manon* and 'Remember the night the night you said "I love you",' and a more 'pop' item, 'I wonder where my Baby is tonight', a normal musical repertoire for a young man of that time.

Sunday was rather a descent after the glories of Speech Day. It seemed to be punctuated by listening to services in Chapel, eating large meals and rushing Ralph back for an awful thing called 'Sunday Lesson' which cut completely into the afternoon and prevented one doing much. We left on Monday morning by a slow and rather shabby local train feeling we had really descended from the heights.

XIII

We Discover the Grange

Among the many problems occasioned by Ralph's going to Shrewsbury was one related to our domestic situation. When Ralph announced that his great friend at Shrewsbury had bought a motor bike and intended coming over to see us one day we were filled with alarm.

Firstly our much cherished new home, though it looked brighter and more charming than the old one, only consisted of three rooms upstairs and three rooms down. It had no bathroom and no indoor sanitation. Our old house did at least have a bathroom even if the hot water supply never worked in it. We were, of course, better off than our neighbours, none of whom even had water laid on and had to carry it all from the Water House near our gate. But our visitor could hardly be expected to know and appreciate this. There was nothing we could do about it.

The second problem which worried us just as much, strange though it may seem in these days, was the fact that we had no maid. Our visitor was the son of a clergyman who lived in a Vicarage home like we did but they did have a general maid and it seemed a terrible social faux pas not to have one in schoolboy eyes. There was a lot of discussion about the matter and even some suggestion of getting someone in to look like one on the day. Then we realised that the boy was just going to turn up any day when the weather seemed good and such subterfuge was not possible so we had to leave these problems unsolved. Needless to say, when he did come he seemed a very nice boy who did not evince any horror or disdain at our simple arrangements and we felt Ralph's alarm had all been unnecessary but social conventions in those days died hard.

Another problem that arose through this new development

of social consciousness was our behaviour when out. My mother had always prided herself on her informality and rather enjoyed shocking the more conventional on many occasions. I think she inherited this from her namesake Aunt Alice whose quick wit and 'racy' remarks disturbed Victorian Society.

My mother used to say, when accused of doing anything unconventional away from home: 'What does it matter, no one knows me?' When she was in her own district she would reply, 'What does it matter – everyone knows me?'

So we children could never successfully restrain this rebel behaviour even when she put us to the excessive embarrassment of saucering her tea in public. She had an iron will and when she decided to do something there was no turning her from it.

Quick cups of tea were a hobby of my mother's. On looking back I think she must have been a snack bar pioneer. When we went on an expedition to one of the Five Towns, our nearest large shopping centre, she would develop a great craving for a cup of tea after exhaustive shopping. As we had so much to do on these rare expeditions, we could only pause to take it just before the bus went, at the local cafe called by the same name as the bus 'The Dorothy', but not in any way connected with it or close to the stop. My mother would never walk sedately upstairs to the cafe, like the local potters' wives, laying their gloves correctly on the table and waiting properly till the white-aproned waitress appeared to ask for orders. Instead she would precipitate a departmental crisis by leaning over the cake counter downstairs, and asking for cups of tea to be sent there from the kitchen, which she knew was just behind the counter.

Her line of approach and her urgency of appeal, backed by a certain firmness known as 'Mummy's Heavy Manner' would finally succeed in achieving her end. A sulky shop hand would go through the swing doors, returning with the required cups and push across the counter at us exasperatedly.

The tea being hot and the time short, my mother would immediately resort to her favourite method of cooling it by saucering it and prevail on us children to do the same. I would generally succumb to this suggestion at last, but only grudgingly as time passed and our departure was imminent. I would become far hotter than the tea as I looked round surreptitiously every now and then to see if there was anyone who knew us in the shop.

One day as I bent thirstily over my saucer I heard a child's shrill voice cry out, 'Oh Mummy, look at those funny Easter eggs all in frills.' This statement was followed by peals of high-pitched laughter. Realising by the silence that greeted this outburst that this was like saucering your tea, something of a social faux pas, I took courage and turned and faced the shop, saucer in hand.

My embarrassment was soon renewed, however, when I heard the lady in charge of the little girl greet my mother as a friend. I turned back to the counter, to try to bury my face in my tea cup, but it was too late, my mother insisted on my being introduced. The little girl's mother was not at all horrified by the situation, however, but amused and delighted at what seemed to her very practical arrangements for obtaining a quick cup of tea.

She rescued her little girl from the Easter egg counter and presented her to us. She had reddish gold hair, a lovely complexion, a small button nose and an impish smile in her large round blue eyes. She was dressed in a large white fur cap and coat and seemed to me a mixture between pictures I had seen of Baby Bunting and a snowy figure on a Christmas cake. I was highly intrigued by her.

Mrs Bernard, as the lady was called, was delighted to hear about our move to the new house. She lived in a nearby village and we had moved in her direction. It was only a two mile bicycle ride by a pleasant country lane to her house, she pointed out. She immediately invited us to a party there on the following Sunday.

This invitation caused great excitement, especially as she was the aunt of the girl my brother was so fond of. The dancing class had been disbanded so we had not met her for some time. She was almost certain to be at her aunt's and I remember my mother counselling me again not to show any surprise or excitement, or tease my brother if this girl should appear at the party, and I promised to observe this.

Mrs Bernard Moore, whom we were destined to get to know very well, was a truly remarkable woman. She was an ardent Catholic and had thought in her early twenties that she had a vocation for the cloister. She went to the local nuns about this matter. But after a period of prayer and thought about it, they refused her request to enter the convent on the grounds that they felt strongly that she had a vocation in the world. She was disappointed but she accepted their verdict and had not long before her true vocation appeared.

Mrs Bernard's elder sister, who was married, died leaving three motherless children. After some time her sister's husband proposed to her. In those days it was very difficult to marry your brother-in-law, but after special arrangements had been made and a dispensation had been obtained from the Pope, she was able to do this and started the task of mothering her two nieces and nephew.

Hardly had she done this, however, than her husband's brother, who was also a widower, died and they decided to take in his six children, making nine in all.

This would not have been a difficult task if they had had economic security, but unfortunately, her husband was an artist rather than a business man. He made history in the creation of beautiful ceramics, but at this point he lost a very large portion of his income through some unsuccessful experiment. She was faced with a great financial struggle which added to her responsibilities.

She had weathered all this, however, and nineteen years after they were married, when her step children were all safely reared, as if as a reward for all her efforts on behalf of other people's children, she had a baby of her own, the small daughter we met her with in the Dorothy Cafe.

We went to Mrs Bernard's party the following Sunday, and to many others that she gave. For us it was an initiation into a whole new group of friends and interests that became of great value to us.

Aunt Mo, as she was affectionately known to all her friends, lived in a beautiful old house called The Grange. It was separated from the road, which ran at the side of the house, by a wide mossy wall and a mature orchard. The rest of the house and garden was encircled by trees and shrubs in uninhibited profusion, and at the other side of the house was a long pool emerging from overhanging trees and stretching away into green fields beyond.

The house inside was a delightful mixture of beautifully displayed old furniture and china, mingling in a sort of comfortable casualness which made one always feel at ease there. It was a home typical of Aunt Mo's personality.

There was a story told of how she went one day to pay a call on a retired naval officer's family who had just come to the neighbourhood. Looking round their house she remarked with usual spontaneity and complete absent-mindedness – 'What a nice house, so like my own, so many muddles.' Unfortunately, the hostess did not appreciate the joke.

I suppose the parties at The Grange might appear a muddle too, to the ultra precise. Actually they had just that ease and impetus in them which kept things going, and the medley of people who came there, happy.

Every Sunday the family attended Mass, being devout Catholics, and then after lunch all Aunt Mo's children and foster children, now married with children of their own, began to drop in, nephews and nieces and friends like ourselves who had received an open invitation to come any weekend.

The place became a maelstrom of family news and bickerings, local gossip (mostly of a benign kind), and amusing stories related by Aunt Mo herself. It was the ideal house to overcome any self-consciousness and sense of social inadequacy such as I suffered from then. Everyone got swept up into the general animation and activity, there were no awkward silences, so even the shyest person felt able to speak to their neighbour under cover of the general hullaballoo.

Activities were provided for everyone's taste and age. Bridge in the drawing room for the older people; tennis for the young; games arranged for the children. There were plenty of places along the up and down dilly lawns and shrubberies where you could walk and chat quietly to a friend apart from the main concourse, if you wished to.

If it was wet and tennis became impossible, the young people repaired to 'The Nursery', a huge wooden room which had been specially added at the side of the house to accommodate all the children Aunt Mo had brought up at

The Grange. Built near the pool, it was rather dark inside due to overhanging trees, but it had a very cosy feeling as one scrambled in from the rain through the raised French Window and faced the glowing fire that always seemed to be burning with the high backed oak seat placed beside it.

There was a magnificent refectory table, and on this stood an old brown gramophone. We put records on this and danced rather self-consciously to 'Always' and 'I Wonder Where My Baby is Tonight'.

I liked dancing the least of all our activities then, for I had not yet learnt the subtle joys of following a partner intuitively in the rhythm of each individual dance. I was still too inhibited by the regimented atmosphere of the dancing class to look anything but intensely worried at the prospect of taking the floor. In consequence of this I was always the last to get a partner. I was often not asked at all, and had to remain perched uncomfortably on the edge of the refectory table toying with some records self-consciously, or sitting by the fire, on the oak bench, my cheeks becoming red, with the effect of the heat I liked to think, but really with embarrassment.

My brother's special friend was always one of the first to get a partner, I noticed. Her success greatly puzzled me, for she seemed to make so little effort to achieve this.

She had now shortened her hair, and wore it in a page boy bob. It was another style that suited her very well for it enhanced her natural dignity. Why, I pondered in my mind, did she attract so many partners when she spoke hardly a word to them, while I worked so hard to be bright and say the right things. I knew little then of the attractions of personality, those unspoken thoughts and subtle human characteristics which are far more magnetic than the bright chatter and platitudes aimed at men which they quite reasonably hate – especially on a wet afternoon when the tennis court has become sodden and dancing seems rather flat in the cold light of day.

As soon as the gong went all activities ceased and everyone converged on the dining room. It was not a very big room but by a miracle it held all the guests, who fitted into one huge table. Every kind of seat had to be pressed into service, including a bench for the younger ones, who could sometimes hardly lift an elbow to reach for the cake.

The tea was always served by a wonderful manservant called Bollington who was a pillar of the family. He was not at all the intimidating butler type, but a pale shy man rather like a ghost, a fact that seemed accentuated by his long black tail coat which he flitted about in hesitantly in the background.

The story went of how one day Aunt Mo sent him out hurriedly to the post in the village. He came back with his face covered with scratches. 'Oh Bollington,' she exclaimed. 'Whatever have you been doing?'

'Very sorry, very sorry, Madam,' he expostulated, 'I met some trees.'

He was much more successful at serving tea than posting letters luckily, and carried out his duties without any apparent accident.

The table was always laden with wonderful sandwiches and cakes but the crowning glory was a huge iced cake in apple green which was the exact replica of a spring cabbage. The source of its origin was a mystery. It was certainly never on sale at the famous Dorothy Cafe, and it was not made at The Grange. Its fantastic unique appearance made it akin to some magic pumpkin that the fairies had placed there themselves.

Tea was the time at which Aunt Mo's husband appeared. As a genius in his own sphere he was rather absent-minded and aloof from ordinary gatherings and sat, stoutish and blue-eyed, at the head of the table, looking quite bewildered by the rest of the company.

Aunt Mo sat at the other end of the table, very much the life and soul of the party. She always looked nice, with charming clothes, but never self-consciously 'posh' or studied, so she did not outshine her visitors and cause one to feel depreciated in any way.

In those days the coat frock was a very popular garment, in a dark colour, usually, with an open front filled in with a white jabot and a thing called a 'Modesty Vest'.

Topless garments had never been heard of in those days but today all modesty having gone regarding a woman's bosom, such an article of clothing has become as extinct as the Dodo. In fact, it may cause some surprise to many people who have never heard of it probably.

I recall that Aunt Mo had a navy frock of this kind, which became her very well. She caused enormous conjecture at one party because when leaning forward to grasp the green cabbage cake, the vest creaked ominously. Quite unembarrassed by this, she explained to a delighted table that she had been unable to find her modesty vest when she changed that afternoon, so she was wearing the laundry list inside out, instead.

The puerile snobberies of haute couture often practised at social events where women gather, were quite impossible in Aunt Mo's circle. That is what specially endeared her to me, I suppose, and helped me to feel at ease in spite of my modest wardrobe.

Aunt Mo kept the conversation going at the table the whole time by relating the fantastic adventures that she seemed to become involved in, in ordinary everyday life.

There was the car, for instance, one of those splendid Baby Austins of other days – plump and small, painted a discreet green, open with a hood to put up in bad weather. A normal little vehicle enough – but what adventures it had gone through. I used to think, when driving with her, that she must put a great strain on the St Christopher medal, specially blessed by a local abbot, which she carried on the car to protect it from disaster.

The most exciting episode of her driving career came after she had attended the ordination of her great nephew who became a Redemptist Father. She was returning down the back drive of the Shropshire mansion called Hawkstone Hall, where the monastery was situated, when the car went into the most frightful skid on a bend in the soft, muddy drive. It rushed madly forward, jumped a three foot wall, and plunged into the estate timber yard. Here its scenic career was providentially terminated by a large piece of wood which shot up somehow and stuck into the vehicle underneath the bonnet, successfully preventing any further progress but without injuring anyone in the car. This was, indeed, a mercy of providence because, as Aunt Mo explained to her spellbound audience at the tea table, in the excitement of the moment she had instinctively reverted to her earlier days, and was under the impression that a car was controlled like a horse, she had been wrenching the steering wheel back with all her energy in the hope of reining it in!

This remarkable car seemed to have a great gift for taking walls in its stride, according to another famous story about it relating to Aunt Mo's husband. He was in his eighties when he asked his daughter, when sitting beside her in the car, how she drove it. Unfortunately she showed him, but as she thought it was just idle interest, she did not tell him how to stop it.

She went into the house to fetch the shopping list, and while she and Aunt Mo were in the drawing room cogitating on shopping problems, they saw the car shoot past the window, take a piece off the bricks at the corner of the house, and charge down the drive, into the orchard, passing miraculously through the maze of gnarled apple trees. Then it jumped up on to the top of the wide mossy wall which divided the orchard from the road and stuck there, intricately wedged some feet up, between the branches of two large apple trees.

Although The Grange was in a quiet country district outside the village, nine strong men suddenly appeared from nowhere, provided apparently by providence, and asked in typical local phraseology, 'Is the party 'urt?' To which the family replied that he did not appear to be 'urt, but he was still up the tree which was very awkward, and could they help to get him down.

They agreed readily, and miraculously produced saws and all the necessary equipment and proceeded at once to the scene. The 'driver' did not seem injured and replied to anxious enquiries passed up to him, impatiently – 'I'm all right, what are you fussing about, get me down.' They did in due course, and both the car as well as its occupant appearing none the worse for their adventure, they all proceeded on their various ways.

Truth is indeed stranger than fiction, and it was adventures such as this that gave such an animated tone to the tea table and kept people amused without rancour or bitterness. It was the kind of humour that was infectious and draws everyone in, even shy beginners like myself, a fact I very much appreciated.

XIV

Expedition to Oxford

When we went to Shrewsbury not only did we have to economise in clothes but also in accommodation.

We could not possibly stay at the famous hotel The Raven, where my parents spent their honeymoon.

We were lucky to find a series of rooms in the town, however. I specially remember a charming pink colour washed house at the Abbey Foregate kept by a certain lady called Miss Barnett, the only one drawback being that it was near a shunting yard. I remember one dreadful occasion when I had to pile into a double bed with my parents because the house was full; none of us slept a wink all night but lay awake listening to the bangs and bumps of the shunted trucks interspersed with the puffings of the engine letting off steam.

There was a pleasant old garden at the back of the house and a long narrow slope running down to the railway line; only the top half was cultivated.

I remember that the wild disorder of nettles and wild flowers in the flower half depressed me in those days. I was so conditioned to the cleared and conventional I suppose but now I should regard it as an interesting habitat and an encouraging effort at conservation.

Ralph took us for a walk there and it was here on the edge of the nettles that he began to tell us that after much thought he had decided to be a doctor. This was a great change as hitherto he had studied Classics and Science known then as 'The Modern Side' was something quite different.

We were all very excited to hear this news, my mother was especially overjoyed. There had never been a doctor in the family for years and as her mother's name was Lister she had always felt a strong link with the medical profession.

So now the time had come to plan a University career for him. The cost of this even in those days was far beyond the modest income of a country parson but my grandmother, who was of course what was known as 'comfortably off' had offered to pay.

This meant that the plan was subject to certain scrutiny not only from Granny, but from that dominating personality, Aunt Nellie. She had other ideas. Like so many women who are frustrated and unhappy, she had undergone several operations. In those days they were episodes of some rarity and drama. If Ralph was to do medicine she felt that he ought to go to Edinburgh where one of her favourite surgeons, now almost a hero, was in residence. Edinburgh had a good reputation as a Medical School of course, but Aunt Nellie had failed to consider the feelings of the family concerned.

My father was dismayed. He had set his heart on Oxford where he and his brothers and his father had all been. I can recall him walking up and down the dining room and saying to my mother, 'If that woman interferes with this!'

But somehow Providence, and possibly my lawyer uncle, intervened and the way opened for us. Oxford was agreed on. Ralph was accepted for Queens, and called to Oxford to do Responsions. In a recklessly extravagant moment we decided to all accompany him and visit that hallowed place, taking a vow beforehand not to let Granny know.

I became so excited about this visit that I immediately got one of my terrible bilious attacks that most children seemed to suffer from then – probably owing to too rich a meat fat diet. The treatment seemed usually to be a dose of whisky, I can't think why. For this reason I have always loathed whisky as a drink. Perhaps it was a forerunner of antibiotics, but it seemed to do little good and generally made me sick. The cure was certainly not instantaneous and every day as the date got nearer I worried as to whether I should be better in time. In those days everyone seemed to be having their appendix out and I was also terrified of this happening to me when I was away from home.

'However, I got on my feet somehow when the day came, feeling wan and rather depressed, not helped probably by my mother's anxiety. My father, who took the illness far less seriously being one of a large family was determined we should all enjoy this great event.

Whenever we went away my father was always filled with schoolboy excitement himself really, but used to try to foist this on to me by exclaiming, 'Now for the Strawberry jam', as the train moved off. 'Look at that girl, isn't she getting excited.' I cannot say on this occasion I responded very warmly to this suggestion, but at Banbury I began to feel much better when he rushed out of the train and purchased a packet of Banbury Cakes, a long promised delicacy and rashly gave one to me. My mother protested at first and then watched anxiously but there were no bad results.

When we reached Oxford, the cultural and architectural delicacies that my father had also promised us further revived me. Rather weak after my illness, with everything sounding far away, I walked up the High in a strange dream which seemed appropriate to the occasion really. Here were all the things Daddy had talked of for so many years actually spread out before us. The great sweep of 'The High' and in those days it was a glorious sweep, unimpeded by islands for pedestrians, labelled 'Keep left' – halfway across it. There was Brasenose where my grandfather had been, and Daddy's smaller College, Teddy Hall, appropriately covered with a wonderful mauve wistaria, which has alas since disappeared. There were the famous stairs at the back by the chaplain's room, where, when sending his dogs downstairs to their kennel late one night, the chaplain and the dogs were terrified to see a man hanging in the moonlight! When the chaplain rushed forward with a knife to cut him down – the vision – of an actual episode in past years, it was later discovered – vanished from sight.

Then, too, in lighter vein there was the window to Taddy O'San's room which Tucker, the wag, had been ragging when the owner returned. He left in such haste that he tried to go head first down the ladder that he had propped against the window but was caught literally by the heels by Taddy O'San. There was the charming little dining Hall where an enthusiastic north country father had committed a dreadful social faux pas in Hall by leaning across the table and saying to his son, 'Ate lad, ate, thou hast paid for they dinner.'

It is strange how the emphasis of the important and the

humorous seem to change with each generation. The Oxford of my father's generation was full of practical jokers. Perhaps they were a hangover from the days when the young beaux were supposed to be audacious and full of clever tricks. They were also the expression of care-free happy days, before two world wars had clouded the sky and made the problems of international affairs and rehabilitation the urgent concern of all thinking people.

But none of these great questions overshadowed us on that day. Here was Oxford, the same as ever and here were we as a family getting the great opportunity to enjoy our discovery of it all together.

I remember I felt so delighted by it all that I was later on moved to write a poem beginning –

Oh what a lovely place it is this lovely May Day morn
The Broad seems full of boundless space and yonder is the Corn.

In those days I was very apt to lapse into verse on some important or moving occasion. The tempo of life I lived was so much slower than it is today, there was room for reflection and the mood suitable for the composure of such things.

On our second day there Ralph started Responsions and went to the Schools wearing a white bow tie, which impressed me very much. While Ralph was thus occupied my Father continued to show us over Oxford. We saw all the usual landmarks, but the most remarkable thing I recall was the unaccountable frescoe of Dean Liddell on the wall behind the altar in the side chapel of the cathedral. It was brought to our notice because my father, who always had an interest in supernatural things, had seen a piece about it in a newspaper. When we asked the Verger who showed us round, about it he said that the imprint had been there for years, but this newspaper man had only just written it up, and brought it to the notice of outsiders.

The frescoe certainly was an amazing sight. There, as if etched in by an artist's hand, or accurately photographed and printed on to the plastered wall was a profile of a very good-looking old man with fine ecclesiastical features and longish white hair. It was said to be a good likeness of the old man, and it had appeared appropriately in the side chapel where the Liddell memorials were. How it got there no one knew. It just apparently slowly developed on the wall. The verger said there was no known explanation of it.

'Oh, there is another one by the door,' he said casually, as if they were an everyday occurrence. 'It is either an old man who used to sing in the choir here or St Peter we are not sure which.'

He pointed upwards and, sure enough, on the wall high up to the right of the great west door was the likeness of an old man with a long white beard looking down on us. This seemed to me doubly convincing that it was a supernatural source, because no one could reach the place to etch it in without using an extremely long builder's ladder.

In later years I have been back and been disappointed to see that both of them have disappeared. So far as I can recall that section of the wall in the chapel has been completely covered by a reredos. Whether the frescoe disappeared or the reredos was put over it cannot be ascertained now. But the wall above the door is still uncovered and unless it has been recolour washed since 1924 when I saw it, the other frescoe must have faded out of its own accord. It is a pity that so far as I know no psychic investigators made a record of these images. Today with the great interest in such things, their cause and origin would have been much more clearly gone into.

We also made some interesting contacts with living personalities. I recall attending Chapel at New College and seeing the famous Dean Spooner. In those days Spoonerisms were very much a part of conversation and we had a full vocabulary of them in our family.

Besides the Spoonerisms there were some delicious stories about the short-sighted Dean (who was of course really an albino) chasing what he thought was his clerical hat dislodged by a gust of wind, only to find out that it was a black hen.

While in Oxford we went to tea with his sister Cathie, who had married a friend of my father's, the Reverend George Inge, who was Vicar of a neighbouring parish until he retired to a house in the Woodstock Road at Oxford.

Mrs Inge had fair whitish hair which was swept back from her brow and coiled up in a large bun at the back, a style which suited her tall figure and gave one ample opportunity to see her profile and charming friendly smile. Her husband was an uncle of the famous Dean of St Pauls known as the Gloomy Dean, but the Reverend George Inge was a much beloved person as the plaque commemorating him as Vicar shows in Beswich Church. He was a saintly old man who appeared to live somewhat away from reality in a world of the classics. There was a delightful story about how with great effort he was organised into getting ready for a visit to the local town, and pushed off to the station with only a few minutes to spare.

The front door had not closed very long, however, before it re-opened and he was seen creeping in to his study. When his faithful wife rushed forward to see what had happened, he remarked with a gentle smile –

'I can't think of the origin of that tag from Tacitus I have in my head. I just had to come back and look it up!'

By this time, of course, the local train which ran quite infrequently, was steaming out of the station.

Like many people of that generation, he did not only excel in the academic world, but also in the athletic one too.

There was a story of how when he was away at the seaside on holiday he was walking along the sea front in one of his reveries when he was sighted by some players on a neighbouring cricket field. One of the teams taking part in a match had turned up short of a player. The situation was urgent.

'Let's ask the parson to join in,' said someone in the team.

They did and he readily accepted. Judging from his appearance he looked rather more a liability than an asset, so the captains agreed to toss for which ever team had him. He duly fell to the side batting first and was put in.

After he had rapidly scored over a century not out and was forging ahead for another, they became greatly puzzled. After a triumphal end to the innings they discovered, to their amazement, that it was a cricketing Blue they had recruited into their midst.

XV

Family Shadow

It was soon after we went to Oxford, however, that the first real shadow came on to our family horizon in the shape of the serious illness of my father. It came as a special shock, I think, because he had always seemed so abnormally strong. In a tough suit of clerical grey he went everywhere, even in a blizzard, laughing at the idea of taking an overcoat. But for some time now he had had some rather disturbing symptoms, which we felt might denote kidney trouble, but this was pooh-poohed by our family doctor, who had known him for so long as such a very healthy man.

'Nonsense man,' he used to say, 'you will outlive me by years.'

Gradually, however, his usually fresh, pink complexion became clouded with a yellowish tinge, and he began to look very ill. While staying away at Uncle Ernest's, he was persuaded to see my uncle's doctor over there, who was not in any way influenced by his previous case history. He took a very serious view of the case.

I have never forgotten the agonies of that first consultation. The doctor had an elegant house in the High Street of the local town. The waiting room, where I was left in suspense for what seemed an interminable time, was furnished in the most perfect taste. It had dark parquet floors with exquisite tallboys, and chests of drawers with big earthenware vases filled with honesty standing on them. I shall never forget the peculiar smell that came from them and permeated the whole room, a clean, bitter smell, sharp and frightening, with nothing in it I could identify but cloves. The whole thing was symbolised for me in those jars, so coldly correct and impersonal, with the silver-grey flowers portraying the living beauty of nature frozen into rigor mortis, while the strange scent spoke of the odour of death.

Patients came and went in the waiting room, and still my people did not appear. I began to think they must have left by another door, and forgotten about me. I was nearly in tears when my mother suddenly appeared, to tell me not to be puzzled by the long wait. They were still there, but my father was being X-rayed. I gathered this indicated the seriousness of the consultation.

I recall that I moved at this point from the scented precincts of the waiting room to the hall, where I sat on an old oak bench by the door. I listened apprehensively to the voices inside the consulting room, catching a word now and then when the doctor raised his voice in a curious way in the middle of a sentence. This only increased the tension. Could Daddy, of all people, be seriously ill? My whole world seemed to be suddenly turning upside down.

Then I recall how the doctor's wife, an immaculate, impersonal person, dressed appropriately to match the house, opened the door of another room on to the hall, and called out to a uniformed maid:—

'Tell Barnes to mark out the tennis lawn, it looks like being fine enough to play.'

This corrected the balance of things suddenly. So personal was my world, I could not imagine that life went on without us in the vanguard. If it was a pleasant summer afternoon, and people were preparing to play tennis, then things must be all right. The doctor could not be going to tell my father he was to die.

I was to learn later that life goes on so very much the same in spite of the tragedies of illness and death, and that is why at these times we often feel very much alone.

The doctor's verdict was not at all conclusive. So it was arranged, through the generosity of my uncle, that my father should go to London to see a Harley Street specialist in order to ensure he got the very best advice. My brother and I were to be left at the Vicarage in the charge of my dear old governess, who was used to looking after the house when we were away.

Somewhat reassured by the fact that my father was getting the best possible medical advice, life began to seem a little less gloomy after they had left. It was quite a new experience being on one's own without parents for the first time, and in some ways a little exciting. When my brother suggested that we should give a tennis party and I should be hostess, this idea very much pleased me. Anything that meant co-operation with him on equal terms was attractive to me, and in spite of my shyness, I seized on the idea of being hostess with alacrity.

Of course, we knew the rudiments of what we ought to do through tennis parties arranged by my mother, but we were determined that this should be not only as good as hers but better. We consulted my mother's cookery book regarding new ideas for sandwiches, and decided to make some that went by the exciting name of 'thunder and lightning sandwiches'. It sounded so dramatic, but we were most disappointed to find when they came to be eaten on the great day that in spite of having followed the recipe most conscientiously, they only tasted like honey.

We bought a box of invitation cards at Mr Peppers, the Stationers, and I wrote these out. Of course we invited my brother's special friend. Though we neither of us mentioned it, we knew that this was really the main reason for the party. We thought her too important to send an ordinary invitation card to, so I wrote personally to her. I remember how carefully we went over the letter in order to sound just the right note, sufficiently keen to bring her along, but not too much lest it frightened her away.

In spite of our care, she refused the invitation, owing to a quite genuine previous engagement I think. How often that happens to the guest you want most. We were very sorry about this, but the party had to go on just the same, on account of all the other people who had already accepted.

I recall finally sitting proudly at the huge oak table, placed in our new house in the bow window of the lounge, with people all round it. It held at least fourteen when full, with dear Miss Slater, the governess, sitting rather bewildered in our midst. She wore a benign smile on her face, which she did her best to maintain amid all the rapid conversations and rather extravagant expressions of 'How perfectly wizard!' 'How priceless,' the current slogans of those days which were bandied about at the table. The climax came, however, when one of my friends rather known for her daring wit, told a story about an old friend we all knew, Auntie Cull, who was unable to attend the party that day.

She related how Auntie Cull on going to bed had found an earwig in her bed. She had fetched a duster, and removed it with great care, and then got into bed. 'Imagine her horror, therefore,' my friend went on to say, 'when on rising in the morning, she found it still there. She had slept with it, my dear. Too improper!'

In those days, when the word sex and all aspects of the subject were not spoken of with the casual frankness of today, this had a definitely shock-producing effect. I recall the expression that spread slowly over Miss Slater's face was rather like the beagle's, when they had suddenly been whisked into a new environment in the doll's pram when being pushed along at great speed.

A few days after this came the news that the doctors still could not find the cause of my father's illness, and they were to perform an exploratory operation. It was the first time that I had heard this extraordinary word, and I was too bewildered by its voluminous size to perceive its literal meaning. So I still felt very much in the dark about the whole matter.

After all the social excitement of the party, and the emotional suspense of Daddy's illness, I developed a super bilious attack, this time accompanied by a high temperature and an appalling rigor which shook me in a terrifying manner from top to toe.

My brother, now a budding medical student, called from his bed in the middle of the night by the faithful Miss Slater, was delighted to find such interesting clinical material right on his doorstep. His commonsense reaction, and Miss Slater's motherly concern, combined with a visit from the family doctor next day, succeeded in bringing about a satisfactory recovery.

Then came the good news that my father had only had his gall bladder removed, that they had found nothing malignant, only an internal catarrhal condition which it was hoped would clear up with time. There was further good news for us. My mother was returning home in order to take us back to London. How excited I was at the prospect of viewing the great metropolis at last. We had, of course, visited several of the larger industrial towns in the midlands, and always when regarding their vast centres I had said, 'Ah, but this is not London!'

When we really reached the great Olympic, unlike Oxford, London seemed something of an anticlimax. I found myself saying, 'This is nice, but London is better,' and then suddenly realising, 'This is London!' I hope I shall not be disappointed in Heaven if ever I get there, for the unobtainable is apt to take on quite a different complexion when it is obtained. But Heaven, I am comforted to feel, is not subject to the limitations of this earthly sphere.

We stayed in rooms in Beaumont Street, a few doors away from my father's nursing home, in a rather rarefied atmosphere where the landlady let rooms to a few qualified doctors and selected post graduates, and occasionally the relatives of patients in the nearby nursing homes.

I shall always remember the kindness of one of the young doctors we got to know there who hit on the wonderful idea of taking us round London to see it after dark. My mother was so easily lost in it she hardly ventured far even in daylight. She would never have dared to do this. What an expedition that was! It will always remain in my memory as a highlight in every sense of the word.

We travelled down Regent Street on the top of a bus, and in those days travelling thus was quite an adventure in itself because the top was entirely open.

Blown and buffeted about, we looked down on an unrestricted view of crowded streets and sparkling lights. At Piccadilly we descended from our giddy perch I recall, and stood and watched the dazzling patchwork of lit advertisements changing with breath-taking rapidity before us. I remember with special delight the inimitable 'Bonzo' lighting his own cigarettes and then throwing the match away and wagging his tail deliciously, at the corner of Shaftesbury Avenue. Then we proceeded on foot to Trafalgar Square, where we saw above Grand Buildings – where my mother and grandmother had often stayed in the quiet seclusion of a famous hotel in earlier years – a resume of the latest news of events all over the world spilled across the sky in sparkling

With Mummy and Daddy

With my parents at the seaside

Mrs Thornton and Mr Thornton,
Lady Bullers' coachman

Dilhorne Vicarage.

letters. Here, at least, I felt that the great metropolis had come up to its reputation as a hub of the universe.

Underneath all this gaiety and excitement and crowds, however, I was aware of a great loneliness during our visit to London that caused a sense of depression. It was the vastness of those streets, and the thousands of strangers who lived in them, that disturbed me. It was all so different to our village where everyone was known to us. I was rootless here, without the reassurance of familiar faces and landmarks. I was terrified of losing sight of my mother, and kept near her all the time. How far was this the outcome of my early childhood and Nanny, and the great love and joy that had surrounded me then?

I had known instinctively from a child that there was this other world containing sorrow and that was why I myself not Nanny had to keep it away by begging her to stop if she sang anything sad or introduced anything that could spoil our atmosphere.

I felt this problem had a deeper psychological aspect too. It was caused by the lack of spiritual and mental landmarks. In the village at home everyone belonged to a small community which in a sense revolved round the church. Even the people who never crossed its threshold did so more from laziness than militant atheism.

In London there were hundreds of people who had actively differing views and were working to destroy the world we believed in. This filled me with terror. I was not yet intellectually competent to face the necessary adjustment of the traditional and modern. I remember looking with horror on the streets we passed down great rows of white houses with long lines of porches, all with classical columns which seemed to go on and on for miles, and all those buildings, I realised, contained people who were strangers and probably antagonistic to us.

Through all this I came to understand the terror of an animal, especially a cat, when it is taken to a new place, and in panic runs miles in order to get back to its old home.

I was very glad, therefore, when my father was pronounced sufficiently well to go away to the seaside. We chose Cromer because of its good air. East Anglia was a part of the world that delighted us all, and filled us with renewed happiness. I shall never forget the sunshine of almost Alpine clarity, and the warmth of golden stubble fields, sprinkled with pheasants in gorgeous plumage in the late August days when we first arrived.

The Norfolk countryside filled me with elation like Oxford had done. I decided to launch into another literary effort, this time one of prose. I still have the MS. It appears to have been a story about a rather comic, Jorrocks-like character whom I pictured owning a farm there. I think my real purpose in writing this, however, was to describe the beauty of the countryside round me which filled me with such delight that I wanted to record it in some way.

I never finished the story, I am sorry to say. I think this lack of perseverance in the literary sphere was due to shortness of time owing to the frequent expeditions we made to historic places, especially churches. My father, in spite of being in frail health, still had a great zest for seeing new things. There was such an amazing wealth of superb churches all around us, the legacy of the days of the wool staplers, but some now left without any pastoral flock. I especially remember one place where we saw two wonderful examples by merely crossing a cornfield from one side to the other. There was not even a hamlet near to justify their existence.

The rich tracery and mellowness of stone in the warm, autumn light was always a visual delight. I remember, too, in what must have been less amenable weather, attempting to munch a sandwich with the head thrown back at the most impossible angle for such an activity in order not to miss for one moment the fantastic coloured patchwork of the roof of Trunch Church, with its flying angels peering down at us, the like of which I had never seen before.

As time went on, and late autumn came, some of our expeditions assumed a more bleak, sinister atmosphere, of howling wind and autumnal decay.

I especially remember a trip to a place called Fellbrigg where there was a strange old house and church standing in the middle of a park. The first thing it was memorable for was the astounding fact that we saw about twelve hares get up out of the long grass round us in the first four minutes after we entered the park. I had never seen one in my life before, so it was an astonishing sight to see this galaxy of rich brown creatures, with their speed and peculiar beauty of movement, flash past, only to be swallowed up in the mysterious forest of long grasses that surrounded us.

The house seemed almost hidden by rank greenery like a house in an enchanted forest. I felt it had an eerie appearance. The Church looked desolate and mysterious, too, with a further enveloping fringe of unkempt trees round it. The chief object of interest in the interior were some fine examples of brasses in the aisles. We had seen a good many of these in other places, and I had thought them beautiful, but somehow at Fellbrigg they took on a special significance as the funereal covering of tombs. I was very glad to leave the little church with its mouldering damp smell of late autumn, and get back into the park, with its wild freedom of bounding living hares and waving grasses.

As we came away, I remember looking back at the house which was some way away from us now across an expanse of unkempt park, and it seemed to bear some of the strange eeriness of Wildfell Hall as we left it to the autumn winds. I little knew that in later years I would get in correspondence with the owner who was a great authority on Norfolk history.

As the months went on, even the town of Cromer emptied, each familiar house lost their jolly, family parties. Figures no longer leant out of the bow windows to call to the children playing ball below. Many of the windows now were curtainless. Sometimes the pale shadows of ghosts of bygone visitors seemed to flit across the vast reflecting fields of the great sash windows. The landladies had retired into their cosy back parlours, even the dogs had lessened in number, many having gone home with visiting owners, no doubt. Even the local dogs lost interest in the outdoor events since the holiday activities had died down. They were curled up by the fireside, instead of essaying trips into the waves after driftwood on the now-empty beaches. The whole front was like some vast, urban skeleton.

Back in the town there was more feeling of life. I remember particularly a small, select little dress shop in a side street where we used to glue our faces to the window, and gaze at the few selected garments placed there as hungrily as if it was a West End mannequin parade. Once, so far as I can recall, we ventured into the precincts, and my mother purchased a Fair Isle jumper for me of cosy cream wool, with a patterned neckband of glorious blue. The vivid colour helped to abate the loneliness and chill that I felt permeated other things.

In spite of having two parents who meant so much to me, and were my constant companions, I realised I had an appalling hunger for human company. Perhaps it was because I was used to being one of a community at the Vicarage. Partly, however, it came from some strange urge to restate myself to someone interested and to explain our family story. Perhaps it was a link with my childish love of telling stories to some imagined listener. Or possibly in that strange maze of human relationships which we are only just coming to know about, something essential is fused by mental contact with other people like recharging a battery.

I can remember to this day the warmth and excitement I experienced when the grandmother of one of Ralph's school friends, the nephew of his housemaster, who kept a shop in the town, asked us in to tea. Our hostess was a redoubtable, stimulating old lady, with one spinster daughter. I recall that I talked far too much and they remarked on it. I felt they were undecided whether it was due to the fact that I was an eccentric or overstrained.

The latter was probably the cause, for I certainly felt very tensed up, as if anything might touch off an emotional crisis. It came in a strange way. It happened that night, when darkness covered the coast, and the wind blew bitterly cold, we heard a rocket explode. Then we saw the lights in the lifeboat house go on, and in what seemed to be an incredibly short time, saw the lifeboat race down the lit runway into the churning blackness below. This was, as it were, the last straw. I was immediately filled with a ghastly terror about being buried at sea, the feeling of overwhelming waters engulfing one. Then I transferred this to an acute fear of being buried alive on dry land. I found out later this was an inherited fear from my grandmother, which was interesting. My overwrought state found expression in this terrifying new idea, and I was unable to free myself from it in our cheerless surroundings in spite of my mother's repeated sympathy and reassurances. I was very thankful when my mother and father came to the conclusion that they must at last make a decision about moving to a new place, and get away soon, as it was too cold at Cromer.

The question was, where should we go? My father would like to have gone to Cornwall, which would have been a place after his own heart, I feel sure. He had read much of Baring Gould and longed to see it. He had an old clergyman friend he wanted to visit there. But alas, our lack of money curtailed our actions once again. It was decided we should make a state visit to Bournemouth, as there Granny would pay.

We took rooms somewhere in a road near Alum Chine, in a dull suburban house a safe distance from the Bath Hotel district where my grandmother still had her rooms, so that we might not be too much involved in her more formal way of life.

Bored by life in Bournemouth, I discovered a new and exciting occupation, however, again taking refuge in my admiration for those who went to sea. It took the shape of watching ships. I did it very systematically. I bought a blue book in one of the shops on the British Navy. Actually, it was selling off at 6d because it was really out of date, but that did not trouble me. A large portion of the ships were still going strong, quite enough to keep me busy.

Every day when the daily paper came I read, as systematically as a man does *The Times* leader, the column entitled 'The Movement of Ships', following with intense interest the cruisers I had never seen, through ports I should probably never know. But in spite of their remoteness, the whole thing seemed to come alive. It gave me an intense thrill to read the words, '*Versatile* arrived at Mombasa', or '*Victory* left for Singapore.'

Apart from this armchair participation in the occupation of the British Navy, I also had a more realistic form of observation. There was a certain garden at the top of Alum Chine which had a fine view out to sea. Here I used to go and stand, with an eagle eye trained on to the horizon, my heart thumping at the tiniest puff of white smoke, of even a cargo boat and leaping with delight when I saw some grey shadow creeping along half hidden in the pattern of churning waters, and knew that the Navy was really passing by. How strongly I felt linked with that great moving entity out there, until I seemed to stand on its decks, and take part in the routine of its community. Often I would imagine myself with the wet, spume-laden air blowing on my face with that full force and freshness that only seems to come when out at sea, speeding along the deck bearing some urgent message for the captain.

Then I would turn from the vast panorama of the grey waters, and regard that other world immediately around me. The pedantic preamblers passing up and down the paths in between the neatly clipped hedges, or fussing about the exact position of their bath chairs, arranged by attentive servants. Even when some of them did pause to gaze out to sea, it appeared to be with a dull, sightless eye, which merely needed something misty and grey to rest on, and was blind to the exciting details of my vast, panoramic world.

Bournemouth in those days was full of depressing sights. It seemed as if every other person was methodically preparing for death, occasioned by old age or chronic illness. In those days, such a luxurious termination to life was possible for most people in the gentlefolk class, providing they had a modest private income. Supported by the faithful servant or companion, (who often gave the best years of their life looking after one exacting person), they could retire gracefully from life and begin this process even in late middle age. Today, the harassed old people, stimulated by new medicines and the hubbub of modern life bereft entirely of servants, keep far more active to the end. It is a harder road, but not necessarily a less happy one. No, Bournemouth in those days was a disturbing sight. I began to feel, surely it was better for those who had died young in the war out there on those ships, for truly 'Age shall not weary them, nor the years condemn.'

My father disliked Bournemouth intensely. He was a lover of real country, and a man of action. Ornamental towns had no meaning for him, since the luxuries of life and social activities were not his choice. If he left the bracing climate of his northern village, it must be for the stimulation of a city like London, or the barren grandeur of the Welsh mountains. I think we mutually hated the endless roads of well-kept villas with their tidy, constricted gardens, and the sleek, purring beauty of the fir trees of Meyrick Park, which spoke of the freedom of nature, but on investigation only revealed a golf course, and the gardens of more stockbrokers' villas.

He felt enervated, too, by the Bournemouth air. He was always tired, yet he could not sleep at all there at night. Much to our disappointment, he had never really recovered his good health; the jaundice and catarrhal condition still went on, and Bournemouth only made him feel more livery.

There were many crises with my mother's family owing to our different ways of life, and certain strange jealousies and criticisms they, in their leisurely life within 'the establishment', meted out to us.

So as soon as the worst of the winter was over, we decided to return home, more determined than ever to remain in the same home and parish, an environment which suited us so well, whatever happened.

The house, of course, was totally inadequate for us, and we had long talked of plans to enlarge it. At first, this had been planned as a Vicarage in co-operation with the various ecclesiastical bodies concerned. But the to and fro-ing of letters and ideas, the visits of diocesan architects and other complications had very much dragged things on, and prevented us achieving our aim for some years. It now appeared, however, important for my father to retire, and therefore we made the suggestion that a new vicarage should be built in the grounds of the Hall, now converted into a miner's institution, and that we should ourselves undertake the tricky work of adding to the small house we lived in. The authorities readily agreed to this. And so we settled down in our own little home in the same parish which we children had lived in the whole of our lives, and seemed to become more wedded to our small world than ever before. Little did we know how the pattern of things would change later.

XVI

A Yorkshire Manor House

In spite of my devotion to our home environments and my idea that I should flounder in difficult situations, I found myself being more and more drawn through a healthy curiosity into new areas of interest. There was also another strong motivating force in my life, the wish to imitate my brother whose activities had widened and gone ahead so through his school life.

It is interesting and encouraging to discover how much many of one's psychological terrors, which appear so impossible to defeat in open conflict, are dispersed when some more dominant interest crops up, the pursuit of which they obstruct. Like a seed pushing its way upwards through hard soil, the mind forces away the obstruction and blossoms forth freely.

This happened when the parents of one of my brother's friends at Shrewsbury asked Ralph to stay with them in Yorkshire, and included me in the invitation because they had a daughter called Ruth also who was about my age.

To my mother's amazement I accepted the invitation straightaway. All my life up till now I had been filled with terror at the idea of leaving my mother, a legacy of those protected days in my early childhood, I suppose.

This invitation however which was linked with an intriguingly new and distant scene, came at Speech Day, an occasion when we were all putting on something of a special show to the world, and I was particularly keen to keep my end up in front of my brother. In this busy masculine community, everybody seemed to talk of going to stay with one another 'in the hols', no one ever thought of the possibility of homesickness, but of the exciting new people and places the host might have to show one.

The next holidays, therefore, Ralph and I set off to pay the proposed visit. My mother was very anxious that we should have the right clothes, to keep us from the chills of Yorkshire and to make us a social success. She found great difficulty to decide what to pack and what to leave out, so we ended up by taking Ralph's large school trunk with almost everything in it. Of course, in those days everyone took more luggage, but I think we did receive some comment from our hostess regarding its size. I don't recall that we experienced great difficulty on the journey with it for it was customary to travel with luggage in those days and there were plenty of porters available.

The journey was a very slow cross-country one involving innumerable changes which made the distance seem far greater than it really was. At Stockport, where we had an hour to wait and went into the town, I felt so desperately homesick I nearly turned back. But the complete inability to communicate this feeling to my brother, with whom I had quite a different relationship to my mother or Nanny, helped me to ignore it and, suffering silently, we boarded the train again. Then I seemed to get control of myself as new landscape unfolded as we sped on towards Yorkshire.

One of the things that supported my frail endeavour most was the fact that I was wearing new clothes. I had never realised before the psychological effect of this. I think I had a suit of some kind, but the garment I recall best was a grey pullover with a V neck outlined by a stripe of pale blue. My mother had bought it at an exclusive outfitter when having lunch with Uncle Ernest in our county town. It really came from the boys' department, but thanks to its pale blue trimmings it did not look over-masculine, only very U and svelt, which gave me a certain feeling of confidence and independence.

My brother's friend, Chris, met us at Bradford, and shepherded us on the local stage of the journey. It was exciting to see the real Yorkshire countryside, and the grey towns with tall chimneys. Finally we arrived at the station of Bingley and after a taxi ride drove up to the old manor house where our hosts lived. It was a charming house, not severe and bleak like some, but set in a valley in a cluster of trees, with pink roses up its sunny south front. Its whole atmosphere was cosy and friendly, and full of an historic past. I remember the stone mounting block by the front door because it seemed to remind me of the cavalier days and my first novel. I could imagine Sir Rupert swinging himself on to his horse or the rustle of silk as his daughter mounted beside him and rode out of the gate.

The family proved very friendly, and we were made to feel at home at once. My namesake, Ruth, had a delightful smile and very friendly blue eyes. They seemed to have an innumerable number of maids clad in demure black dresses and beautifully starched snowy white aprons. They were all one family and had the rosebud complexions of the Yorkshire country girls. They regarded their employers respectfully, but had somewhat the same relationship as Nanny had with us like family friends, so I did not feel alarmed or intimidated by them. They were, I suppose, what we should now call a family of treasures, now extinct, but we did not recognise this in those days, but accepted as a matter of course the cosy punctual domestic scene of which they were the lynch pin.

The family's way of life was so very different from ours, punctual and well organised. They, too, did a great deal of Church work, but in a different way. Innumerable people did not call at all times of the day, and even night, unannounced. Our hostess belonged to many committees, especially to do with the building of church schools and she was also a member of the Church Assembly. Ruth and her mother were very good at sewing and handicrafts. It was here that I learnt how one can turn old sugar bags into colourful dishes of papier maché to sell at bazaars, and many other handicrafts, the materials and instructions being supplied by a special craft shop in London.

Sewing was their great accomplishment, and it was here that I learnt the charm of sitting round in a family circle being read to while everyone plied their needle to something interesting and colourful.

It was strange that our hostess should choose *The Story of the Kirstin Laverens Datter*, by Sigfrid Undset and thereby give me my first glimpse of life in Norway, a country which was to mean so much to me in later years. It seemed very in keeping with our surroundings, this story of the great mediaeval manor house, read in the oak-beamed parlour of a manor house in Yorkshire Dales, a country so full of place names and historical landmarks of the Viking occupation and the great farms they built there. We went out, too, on expeditions because Chris, my brother's friend, had a car – I suppose we should call it a vintage car nowadays. It was, I think, an early Standard, but I don't think the make was ever mentioned because it had an individual personality of its own. It was called appropriately 'Cantering Katie'. Inside the engine was some sort of rubber tube which was meant to link on to part of the engine but kept on coming loose. Ralph and Chris were always trying to tie it on with string but it never worked for long. As soon as they had fixed it up we used to rush into the car and go tearing off up hill and down dale until the rough moorland roads shook it loose and we came to another abrupt standstill.

These enforced stops, however, gave me a wonderful opportunity for observing the beauty of the countryside, while the boys had their heads in the bonnet, absorbed in the problems of the merely mechanical.

I came to love the bleak moorland ridges and the grey towns with tall chimneys nestling in the valleys. In later years when I read more of Emily Bronte, I understood her lonely sorties to those heights and how something there spoke to the depths of her tempestuous spirit.

We returned home from Yorkshire at the end of that brief week having discovered a whole new landscape and environment. I had even obtained a new name in order to avoid confusion with the two Ruths, Mrs Ackroyd suggested I should be called Ruthella, a name I still bear to this day. The seeds of independence had now been sown.

To my mother's amazement I asked if I could go away to a boarding school, my only condition being that it was a public school with separate houses, and house matches and the glamour of a famous name, such as my brother enjoyed at Shrewsbury.

XVII

I Go to School

As I was nearly fifteen years old there was no time to be lost in finding a school for me. Of course we were exceedingly poor, as we still only had my father's stipend as a clergyman, but Uncle Ernest with his great liberality, agreed to shoulder my school fees as Granny had done Ralph's.

I felt specially drawn to a public school where my cousin, Dolly, had been educated. She was one of the first pupils to go there after it was founded and had been academically very successful. This relationship was to prove a useful link later on.

We wrote for a prospectus of the School, and I immediately fell in love with it through the picture on the cover. It showed a huge library window with mellow stone tracery, looking out on to velvet lawns and tall trees. It seemed to come alive to me in a way that none of the other schools we got brochures from did. I could imagine myself sitting in the window looking out on this view surrounded by mellow brown books containing the riches of Elizabethan Literature. Somehow it symbolised to me the flower of these things and the vast field of academic attainment.

In reality I glimpsed the library only once when I reached the school. It was reserved for the Sixth Form. Owing to having learnt scarcely any maths or French, I remained most of my time in Lower Sixth 'Special'. But I was not to know that and the photo gave me something to hold on to and to make me convinced that this was the school I wanted to go to.

We made several expeditions to what my mother thought, perhaps wisely, were smaller, less exacting institutions, more suited to 'a tender plant'. But to me they all seemed mere child's play, embracing parodies of the academic institutions.

The school which I had chosen was the only one I could really believe in because they followed the pattern of the famous boys' schools, and seemed therefore to be all part of the established world.

I was to learn later that although the system generated energy in difficulties and initiative for leadership and the pupils rose to the highest academic heights, there were many things which it lacked for a girl. If only it could have included some of the feminity and emotion that the convent schools seem to manage to incorporate into an equally traditional background linked with discipline, we should have left school better balanced people, able to take our place more easily in a world that consists of both men and women.

On our first visit to Oxford as a family we had stayed, as an economy, in some very dull rooms rather on the outskirts of the town. My mother and I on this second visit to Oxford to see my school, were very extravagant and stayed at a little hotel in the Iffley Road. I had hardly ever seen the inside of an hotel before and it seemed tremendously lavish, all white paint and cosiness which I think denoted central heating – very rare in those days – and very different to our austere vicarage life.

I still recall with what excitement and energy we set forth in the morning. The beauties of Oxford were all round us. Ralph was already studying medicine at Queens, and I myself was on my way to my future school. Already I felt almost part of the hurrying academic population. Truly the world seemed full of opportunities to me now.

We took a train to the town where the school was situated. At the station which stood on a steep hill, my mother asked a porter if it was far to the school. He made the surprising reply, 'You can roll there, madam, in five minutes'.

Needless to say, we did not adopt this suggested form of locomotion, but straightening our hats and trying to look our best for the ordeal before us, we set off down the hill. At the bottom of it we crossed a teeming main street, and then came suddenly into a quiet road, with almost country conditions, a bridge, and a winding stream with trees along its banks. Ahead a barrier of wooden palings faced us, and, opening a door in them so unobtrusive it looked like a panel in a wall, we stepped inside, into another world.

I remember it rather took my breath away, there before us stood the verdant lawns I had seen in the picture, stretching away to a lake which I had never glimpsed before, with gardens running down to the edge of it. To the right was a building of light grey stone with green ivy up the side, and mock gothic towers rather like the illustrations in a childrens fairy story. The sudden transition after the busy market town amazed me. It was indeed a world apart. This was one of its greatest drawbacks, of course, but I was not to know that then.

We hurried up the drive, and after ringing the front door bell and waiting apprehensively, we were ushered into a large entrance hall with pure white walls, high vaulted with a minstrels gallery, and hangings and carpets of rich madonna blue. Its colour scheme delighted me, it seemed so alive and welcoming and right, yet it almost awed me. I felt I had found my right milieu at last.

I was not to know then that the entrance hall was a kind of holy of holies and that I should scarcely ever glimpse it again during my school career, only perhaps at some apprehensive moment on the way to the headmistress's room, when its scenic beauties could not possibly be absorbed. Then later, visiting the school as an old girl, I should drink coffee there, served with tea spoons with horribly over-weighted handles that kept descending from the saucer to the floor with a crash directly you became engaged in any worthwhile conversation, destroying through this social faux pas any composure that one might have acquired since leaving school.

The Head Mistress, who was a New Zealander, was quite unlike the proverbial ogre. She had pure white hair, waving back from her temples, and intensely blue eyes which matched the colour scheme of the hall beautifully. Her eyes were both friendly and challenging. She had the great gift of blending sympathy and authority, which stimulated you and enabled you to be your best.

After the interview my mother wrote home to my father: 'You always said "Blue Stockings" were so horribly plain, but I have found brains and beauty together at last.'

The Head Mistress suggested that as I was so old I should start at school the following term, and offered me a place without delay. This was amazing to us as we had always heard that they had a waiting list there, and that it was difficult to get in. I never knew why she did this. Perhaps it was the connection with my cousin, who was well known to her as she had been in the Head Mistress's own house. Or perhaps it was because she saw in me latent qualities which had not had a chance to blossom forth, and realised that this opportunity would mean far more to me than many more conventionally successful girls on her list.

Of course we accepted the offer, and as it was late autumn we returned home and began hastily buying school clothes, and the general paraphernalia needed to equip me for this exciting new phase in my life.

How proud I was of that uniform because it belonged to a famous school. I must have been an awful little snob in those days. I remember how much I looked forward to wearing it in the holidays so that people would notice and know where I came from.

How disappointed I was later to find that to be seen wearing one's uniform, unless actually coming or going from school, was a terrible social faux pas. If anyone was seen doing it during the holidays, the person who came across them would retail it as an item of great interest to some friend, who would be sure to reply –

'How extraordinary, my dear, was she really?' in a tone of horrified surprise, almost as if the poor girl had been seen stark naked. But these were truths I found out later.

January came in due course and in my unbecoming uniform I plunged into the scholastic maelstrom of 300 girls, a community in which I was to be hopelessly outpaced, bewildered, constantly lost, but never quite defeated.

I think my greatest difficulty in adaptation came from the different tempo of life and the fact that I had been living in a subjective world. Now I found myself in an extremely objective one, always moving at a horrific pace towards some organised goal, a goal for which I often had no enthusiasm at all.

It was not only this need to keep pace with actual physical time which irked me I found so difficult to adjust to, but also to adjust on the mental sphere. Time had only intruded on my life and directed my activities when I cared to let it. I found it intensely frustrating to be forced to thrust away some interesting and creative trend of thought in order to rush off to a 'lesson', which I felt taught me nothing in the deeper sense of the word.

Gradually my mind seemed to become more and more preoccupied with the mundane problems of mere existence and the fear of consequences should I forget something essential for daily routine, so that I failed to enter deeply into anything in the mental sphere.

I particularly remember one day when I was supposed to be piano practising, pacing restlessly up and down in the boot room where the piano stood and gazing hungrily out of the window at a golden summer afternoon fast receding. That day seems photographed in my memory as the day I specially rebelled against the way the ordinary world lived and put on record my realisation of its crude destruction of much of the greatest value in life.

The spontaneous enjoyment of such things as walking on a hillside when the sun was at its best, or rushing out to see the landscape when the woods were filled with subtle blue lights before the sun went down, all these experiences which at home I could grasp at any moment that Nature displayed them, were now denied me, through the intrusion of the organisation of life.

But even if the sun shone or the landscape looked beautiful after work was over, I was denied the enjoyment of these things, for walking alone on 'The Heights', the high land above the school, was taboo for to be alone was considered to indicate that you were unpopular, a slur everyone wanted to avoid. If I defied convention and went alone, then the feeling of prying eyes criticising my strange action inhibited any train of thought I might be wanting to follow.

The only person who ever dared to walk there by herself was my form mistress, who taught English. But then, she wore a long cape and was said to write poetry. Which put her quite beyond the pale of the normal. She was thought to be quite eccentric, some girls adding a sympathetic rider to their verdict by saying: 'She lost her fiancé in the war, you know', as if the shock had made her mildly mental.

This feeling of frustration stimulated to a certain extent my poetic gift as a compensation, I suppose, and it blossomed forth with one or two poems of a rather sad, regretful kind. One of these I ventured to send to the school literary *Review* which was published periodically.

I particularly remember one morning when after form meeting which took place at the beginning of the day, my form mistress, the poet who wore the cape, asked me to stay behind in order that she could speak to me.

I approached her in fear and trembling, quite certain that I must have made another blunder from her stern expression, but on the contrary she was apparently so impressed with the quality of what I had written that she could not believe it came from a shy little pupil like me. Her searching looks and questions made me aware that she thought the thing might be a hoax but when she had established the authenticity of its author she was obviously very surprised! The poem was duly published in the select *School Review*.

To me, the school work was fascinating because it opened up so many new facts of knowledge. As I had had so little consecutive education, and been predominantly self-educated by reading books of the kind I personally enjoyed, I had an enormously healthy appetite for exploring new spheres academically. It filled me with a great sense of adventure.

My classmates, however, seemed endowed with a sense of jealousy. Bored by their environment, they had the mentality of a chicken run, and any unusual bird must at once be set on and pecked. I was good at writing essays and, although my mother had previously expressed a fear that I might appear deplorably ignorant about the Old Testament, I found that I generally came out top in Scripture essays. So my companions spread a rumour round that I was going to be a missionary, because that was a despised profession in their eyes.

The form was not an important unit, of course, in a school, which was planned in residential houses. We only met together in our form room at regular intervals. We scattered into different grades for subjects such as French and Maths, etc. These were held in different rooms all over the school. This was a very disturbing experience for me because I always seemed to miss the room where my class was in some extraordinary way, and turn up harassed and late. It was a terribly difficult school for the absent-minded. If you were a member of one of the outhouses, as I was, and forgot a book, you had to choose between rushing back for it up eighty steps, or somehow doing without it. I was faced with this problem so constantly that I took to putting almost my whole locker into the large brown bag with which we were equipped for use as a school satchel. But then, in my anxious rush from room to room, I found myself very handicapped by an appallingly heavy load.

The House was our chief unit for communal activities and personal friendships. As I was going to school so late, it had been thought advisable to send me to one divided into houses rather than an upper and lower school, because a house, like a college, brought together people of varying age and points of view. I found, however, that in actual practice this was anything but so. We had a very definite dividing factor called 'House order'. It was based partly on the term you came to school, your form, and probably the house mistress's opinion of you, and her wish to accelerate or retard your progress towards the monitorial heights and responsibilities.

Once a day, when we assembled to hear notices given out, and inform the House Mistress what we intended to do that particular afternoon, standing in a circle round the house study, its visual pattern was portrayed. The order was so rigidly enforced as a form of seniority that you could ask no one even a place above you to walk with you up from the main block to your house, or accompany you to a school concert or lecture. As it was essential to have a companion on all these excursions, to go alone was to be thought unpopular, a very real problem arose for any new girl if she came to school late and was near the bottom, like I was.

This system, introduced when the school was founded, was to enforce respect in the girls for their elders and betters, I suppose. It might have been a good preparation for some of the professional institutions, where something of a military system operates.

At school it had a bad effect in that it caused people to take up hasty partnerships for fear of being left out. These almost amounted to the inevitability of a permanently married state.

They precluded one from mixing with the other girls, or attending a function with different companions, and having an intelligent discussion with other girls with different points of view. I do not know, however, that this latter opportunity was missed by the many girls, as a very large proportion below the Upper Sixth seemed to take a very worm's-eye view of life. We had little encouragement from our staff to behave as adults. We seldom saw them apart from lessons, and regarded them mostly with awe and even dislike in some cases. Our House Mistress met us at meals, of course, but she seldom discussed much with us other than the weather. Most of us were too intimidated by her to ever engage in a conversation on deeper matters. She was a very stern Scots lady with a disapproving eye, but it must be said to her credit and our amazement that she became transformed into a human being apparently after she retired by becoming a member of the M.R.A.

Certainly, when people had once found a satisfactory partner for their school career there, it took a great deal of the strain out of life, like finding a reliable husband or cook. The regime then ran smoothly. Most important of all, it eliminated that dreadful 'soliciting' for 'a side' (as sitting next to a person was called), which one had to do before each event if one had no permanent partner.

I would have been quite willing to go alone to a concert of course myself. In fact, I would have enjoyed listening to music alone far more than with an uncongenial partner. But if you walked into the school hall unaccompanied, and tried to find a free place, it was almost as embarrassing as arriving at a large ball without a male escort. In vain one tried to slip into a seat unnoticed, but whichever place you chose, it was always one which had already been 'bagged' by someone for a friend and one moved on like an unwanted beggar amid the protests of the 'bagger'.

When at last, however, the flock had settled, like a lot of chickens, the pecking was over, and the music began, an extraordinary change would come over everything and everybody.

Music was the one subjective art affecting the emotions which it was considered normal to respond to then. While the poet was considered someone rather eccentric, confined to 'strange' people, like my form mistress who walked alone on The Heights, the musician's sanity was never questioned. I don't know what people would have said if they had heard then the story of the great Beethoven how, cut off from this world of physical sound, he touched supernatural heights, and threw his breakfast tray back at his landlady one morning, crying, 'Madam, take it away, I have been wrestling with the spheres all night.' Such temperamental outbursts would probably have put him quite beyond the pale.

Yes, something came over the school as they sat there in a united effort of appreciation – though doubtless at varying levels – even the more dense were passive as they listened, all sitting like some gigantic cloud in their white frocks, tier upon tier, their faces turned intently to the platform. Liberated now from the constraints and terrors of school routine, the need to push as hard as they were pushed, a change seemed to come over each individual. As the music surged up to the raftered roof coloured with heraldic designs, the personal symbols of the family who had previously lived and worked out their life there, it seemed to me that we stepped out of temporal time. What was in store for each one of us? Each young face looked so full of exciting promise, and the high plaintive note of strings seemed to emphasise the triumph of life beyond all the sorrows and difficulties of our daily existence. Suddenly the world of the future lay open before us full of promise and vitality. But though I felt a deep conviction of these things I had no friend with which to share them.

My loneliness at school was relieved somewhat, however, when a barrister's daughter arrived called Prunella. She was about my own age, and had something of my own background. She, like me, had been permitted to enter an adult world early, for she had been the frequent companion of her father, with whom she had a deep affinity. He had died suddenly a little while before, which had been a terrible blow to her. Her mother had thought, mistakenly, that it would rouse her from her grief if she sent her away to a good stimulating boarding school of the tough variety. She did not realise that Prunella, having travelled a good deal and developed her mind through her father's close companionship, was years ahead of almost all her companions.

She arrived late in the term, which made things even more difficult for her. My House Mistress, evidently realising we should have something in common, called me up to her room and asked me to look after her, the first task of any kind she had ever assigned to me. I found Prunella a companion after my own heart, her friendship with her father, her bereavement, and her outlook on life made her see things at a deeper level. It was clear, however, from the first, that she was totally unsuited to the kind of school she had been placed in, so her stay was only short-lived. Finally, she prevailed on her mother to send her to a school in Switzerland instead. So, to my sorrow, I was left alone once more.

A little later, however, another but more tempestuous character appeared. She had also come late to school, and had considerable maturity coupled with a great independence of character. Clare was her name. She was in rebellion against the entire school system, and was always planning to run away. It was amazing that, forthright as she was, she never actually did so.

I listened sympathetically to Clare's troubles, which were more concerned with our daily living than the deeper, more spiritual problems of Prunella. She had such strength of character, however, that she carried me along with her, endowing her problems with a convincing urgency and importance when she spoke of them.

Clare had a very considerable effect on my emotional life, not because I was ever 'cracked' on her, the term then used for one schoolgirl's admiration of another, but because of the traits in her character, some of which harmonised with mine, and some which stimulated me by showing my weak spots. She, like me, had remained an individualist through having grown up in the greater freedom of education at home. She had not been over sheltered, as I had, so she was ready to do battle with anyone who opposed her. By this she suppressed criticism, and gained the other girls' respect in spite of her differing views, in a way I could never do.

For some months after I gained her friendship I was borne along in a state of blissful achievement not only by this sense of being no longer alone, but of belonging to someone who was in the forefront rather than the back of life's cavalcade. My parents had always been over-modest, they 'liked to take a back seat', as my mother always described it. My rather sheltered upbringing had rather accentuated this tendency in me. Being the one who was always left out in a crowd, I became so often unavoidably saddled with some other social outcast as a companion. But now things in my world had come together at last, the individualist was in the forefront, no longer trodden underfoot, and I could identify myself with this because it was my personal friend who had achieved this.

The success of my discovery left me amazed but distrustful of it inwardly because I felt it was all too good to be true. But outwardly I seemed on top of the world.

After some months, Clare began to discuss quite openly with me her wish to link up with another girl, one that we both liked, if only this girl could get free from the person she was going about with. Quite a few people went about in threes, and as I had no sense of jealousy, I imagined this was how she intended to solve the problem, and I was quite ready to accept this other girl into our circle. She had a very creative mind, she wrote poems sometimes like me, and I thought we should have much in common.

That first friendship with Nanny had so established a sense of integrity and security in human relationships that I never even considered the problem that would arise if Clare 'chucked' me. It was beyond my comprehension that anyone would take a friend up and then fling them aside, like a child does an inanimate toy.

The School touched a high spot in its cultural activities that summer with the production of a Masque on the level just outside the Library window. At last my longing to read and make contact in these surroundings with the poetic riches of the Elizabethan age was satisfied. No longer need it be limited to the usual classroom post mortem. How well I recall, for instance, during one of our literature lessons with all its horrors of dissection and the labelling of masterpieces each dismembered part in a Century Binder, realising suddenly afresh the glories of Richard's famous speech,

> For God's sake, let us sit upon the ground
> And tell sad stories of the death of kings.

Not daring to share my enthusiasm with any living soul lest I was thought 'sloppy', I poured it out into the inanimate environs of that brown text book, writing in the margin in large letters 'Magnificent'. What psychometrical vibrations revolved round that word when, years later, I looked at it again.

Here at last, however, on a lovely July night, the poetic grandeur of the age of the Sydneys was unblushingly poured out on the greensward of The Level and all before the library window where I had first felt the urge to reach out to that period of history.

I had never heard madrigals before. I remember with what breathless wonder I heard the clarity of young, unaccompanied voices drifting across the lawns in the opening chorus of the masque:

> Hark! hark! the lark at heaven's gate sings,
>   And Phoebus 'gins arise,
> His steeds to water at those springs
>   On chalic'd flowers that lies;
> And winking Mary-buds begin
>   To ope their golden eyes:
> With everything that pretty is,
>   My lady sweet, arise!

Truly, Heaven's gate seemed open wide for me. The purpose and vitality of life shone so brightly through the chronicle of that early May morning that I seemed to share in it and forgot the barren chaos of the modern world around me.

I recall that after this glimpse of the glories of the sun, the chorus of the masque portrayed a more sinister and shadowy side of nature in the shape of the famous chorus of scorpions, newts, and other unpleasant creatures clad in strange-spotted attire, who wriggled about in gloating horror. It was inevitable that Clare should appear on the Level at this juncture. It was, as far as I can recall, the very point at which she began to ignore me.

It came as a terrible shock when I spoke to her as usual and she stared at me blankly as if she had gone out of her mind, and passed on. Mystified by this, I followed her up to see if she was quite well, only to find she doubled and sneaked round the bushes like the evil creatures we had first seen in trying to shake me off, and refusing even to look at me. She showed not the faintest reaction to the questions I put to her. She might have been stone deaf by the blankness of her face. Then it suddenly began to dawn on me. She had had me for a friend as long as she needed me. Now she had a better one, so she put up a facade like a stone wall. To my entreaties for an explanation she was as deaf as a corpse. I don't recall that she ever spoke to me again throughout the rest of our time together in the same school.

Years later, when I was buying some material at a famous store in Sloane Square, I was attracted by a familiar ring in the hard, tense voice of a well-bred looking woman beside me. I looked up, and then I saw unmistakably the familiar features. There was still something of the challenging, arrogant look in her eyes, but this was clouded now by a strange film of unhappiness which seemed to have come over them during the ensuing years. I listened with interest to her conversation with the shop assistant, like someone hearing a classic tune from the days of his youth. She gave her order and then she went her way, never realising that I had stood beside her and travelled suddenly back over this bridge across the years.

It was only appropriate that the sweet and the bitter should be mixed, and that I should be brought face to face with the reality of the immediate. To experience anything of value, the two must be mingled together.

I would not like it to be thought because I have been concerned here with my adolescent search for the perfect and infinite that I wanted only to gaze into some rarefied picture of the past, and hated my old school for its preoccupation with the toughness of life in the modern world.

I have never ceased to be grateful for the self discipline, integrity and endurance it taught. In an age of rapid communications, when everyone seems to be preoccupied with how to get to the top, either in their job, or even in the spiritual sphere, by every form of short cut possible, I never forgot the truth of those qualities I was taught in my school. I constantly stress them to the younger and more impatient, who seem to think there is no obligation to endure and to earn things in life.

Although I disliked some of the school system, I revelled in the traditions, especially those which pertained to games captains, or similar leaders, because it satisfied my need for a hero. But when I came away into an ordinary world where these things did not count, it meant I had to start seeking outlets for my emotions and directive purposes over again. This caused me a great deal of psychological difficulty in my late teens and early twenties, but this belongs to another part of the chronicle.

I see now it would have been better to have directed this initiative and appetite for toughness and endurance not against the opposing lacrosse team but the barriers of nature, much as the Gordonstoun system does today. This would have been outside the narrow school environs and ideologies and given one something to use throughout one's whole life.

Perhaps it is because of this continuity this universality of nature that, although I am ill at ease in the social environment of my school even now, I still feel a deep affection for the physical beauty of it in the grounds and landscape.

I came to be glad that fate took me so often to the school sanatorium with bad colds for a week or more, because it gave me a chance to step out of the maelstrom of active school life, and reflect on my surroundings.

The building used as a sanatorium in those days looked on to a magnificent tulip tree. It was as individual and as strangely wrought as a piece of antique furniture. I can see now the soft bloom of silver moonlight on grass of the lower slopes leading up to the Heights and in the foreground the strange shaped branches of this great tree which came right down on to the ground.

The loneliness and peace would be broken only by the staccato cry of the Little Owls, peculiar to Bucks! yapping like restless puppies as they moved from bush to bush. Then the school clock would chime, its leisurely melodious tunes spilling out on the night air. And I would lie back on my pillows, joyously secure in the thought that all the hours of the night were mine in which to absorb all this, that no jarring bells or marshalling females would break abruptly into them. What contact seemed to come with the eternal now, what poems to be written, and future fame attained! That these rosy aspirations of personal immortality faded with the dawn did not matter, for I was aware that underneath it all was the reality of the universe, far beyond my personal achievements.

It was, strangely enough however, in the midst of school life and activity that I had the most astounding experience of this reality. Gazing out of the window of my House during evening prayers at the distant Heights topped by beech woods, I said, 'Everyone is in now for prayers, they must be quite empty now.' Then suddenly an overwhelming impression came to me that the hill was not empty at all. No one frequented the woods, or followed the winding path over the Heights, but right in the very heart of the hill beneath all this there was some vast, pervading power which I could not properly describe in any known terms of normal experience. It was a living presence, but it was not a human personality confined in the small area of a physical body, it was universal. It pervaded not only the Heights, but all the other hills round. I knew suddenly that I would never feel alone again on a hillside ever again if I could only capture for ever the awareness of this Great Thing within the heart of the earth.

What puzzled me most was the fact that I had never felt it before. But perhaps the most convincing fact about its supernatural origin is that I cannot feel it now. I can only tell myself and other people about it like a guide describing a building which once stood on a particular site. To me it has become a special moment of revelation that seemed to be one of time.

I know that this is not a unique experience, in fact, if it is an existing spiritual reality, then it would never be limited to the consciousness of one person alone. I have read since of a famous Indian who had the same revelation. It changed his whole life. Perhaps the Indian mind was more fertile soil for spiritual experience, or perhaps he was filling his particular vocation. Sometimes I feel guilty that it did not bring about a more dynamic change in me. I am concerned lest my subconscious self may have said after this great experience like the people in the gospel said when they felt the dynamic power of Christ, 'Depart from me, for I am a sinful man.'

There were, of course, other landmarks on my spiritual road which came to me through other human beings I met rather than my own inner experience. We were in the habit of having visiting preachers who came to a Sunday night service held in the school.

The first to disturb what you might call the stagnant spiritual surface of my soul was the famous wartime Padre, Geoffrey Studdart Kennedy, better known as 'Woodbine Willie'. His fiery challenge, put out with an Irish warmth had a most profound effect on me. He was so completely dedicated to the Christian cause, and in his teaching he translated heroism and devotion, the qualities I had come to admire in war, into the spiritual sphere.

It is because of this that I feel on looking back now that Woodbine Willie and his contemporaries were specially sent to bridge a gap caused by inevitable historical change from the old loyalties, the patriotism of a great Empire, within which religion, as we knew it, had become deplorably mixed up with the status quo, to the true meaning of Christianity as a gospel of international co-operation and brotherhood.

It was only those who had seen war at close quarters in stark reality who could come to fully realise the horrors and the futility of it. Dick Sheppard lived to lay the foundations of a vast movement of re-education in international affairs, and a new interpretation for Christians of the obligations of love towards one's neighbour.

Woodbine Willie died younger, leaving behind him only vivid memories for those who had met the impact of his dynamic character in person as I did, or read his books and poems.

For me the core of his teaching will always be memorialised in the words of his poem:

> Bread of Thy body give me for my fighting,
>   Give me to drink Thy sacred blood for wine.
> While there are wrongs that need for me the righting,
>   While there is warfare splendid and divine.

The sacramental principle of life, the dedication of all the whole of life to God. I had found another piece to fit into my jig-saw puzzle of the meaning of life and which seemed in harmony with that total feeling of caring that had been the character of my early environment. It was probably part of the pattern worked out for my own personal life developing for the next personality whose spiritual impact I felt was one to whom the sacrament was the essential principle for his work and life.

Our Sunday night services in the school hall were always rather cosy affairs. The place was laid out like a simple chapel with an altar with blue hangings, and a fine bishop's chair. There was a first-class piano on which one of the staff played appropriately 'cosy' music.

I remember, therefore, how suddenly the climate seemed to alter one night when a dark-eyed young man rose from the episcopalian chair, and started to speak. He stood, I suppose, well over six feet, and his early training in the Navy had given him a very upright bearing. But the most important thing about him were his eyes, so penetrating and challenging that you could not avoid their gaze.

Father Huddlestone, writing in a church periodical some time ago, related how one of his most vivid memories was as a boy being taken into All Saints, Margaret Street, for Evensong, and seeing for the first time the gloriously lit high altar, and in the pulpit a dark-eyed young man who preached with such dynamic power that he never forgot him.

This was Father Basil Jellicoe, of slum clearance fame. Through his influence, I too was later to know the glories of All Saints, Margaret Street at Evensong, but even in the simple surroundings of the school chapel, the impact of his personality had the same unforgettable effect on me.

In some of the more sleepy and exclusive cathedral towns, it was his practice to take a box of dead bugs with him and tip them out on the rostrum when he began to speak, saying, 'These came from the stately homes of England!' In the cosy life of such places this no doubt came like a cold shower.

In a young community like ours, however, such explosives were not necessary. His presence, bearing and passionate belief in his message were enough to hold the school's attention all the time he spoke.

Years later, when we got to know his parents after his

death, we filled in the background of his remarkable personality. He was the son of a saintly old country parson and a handsome mother with a great deal of Scottish charm. One of Basil's ancestors, she told us – I believe it was a grandfather – had been an inveterate gambler, and lost all the family money and property in Scotland. Basil, she felt, had inherited something of this trait, but used it rightly to gamble with faith instead.

Certainly he gave a clear example of this when he first began his housing venture in St Pancras. The whole scheme hinged on purchasing an empty site occupied by a derelict brewery in order to build some entirely new houses, into which the first group of families could be moved and then begin the whole programme of slum demolition. So much hung on it. The price was £27,000. Father Jellicoe lodged £7,000 with the lawyers, and told them that the rest was being prayed for. Only he could have given these practical legal men the confidence to accept what must have seemed to them a preposterous suggestion. But he was right. After some days of prayer before the Blessed Sacrament at Pusey House and in many other quarters, the money came pouring in. The gamble on faith had been rewarded. And so, 'yet another dark spot that has long been an insult to our Lord was removed', as he put it with that wonderful personal phrasing which made the work seem so urgent and rewarding. The foundation stone laid by his cousin, Admiral Jellicoe, had appropriately inscribed on it, 'To the glory of God and the *hospitality* of His children.'

I suppose that the feelings roused by the descriptions of the slums by Father Jellicoe might not have found a practical outlet had not our very closed school community allowed one glimpse of the real world. It was a brief encounter but it made a permanent impression on some of us.

Like most of the other big schools mine belonged to the United Girls' School Mission. This meant that on one Saturday in each year in the summer term the exclusive gate in the brown palings were flung open and hoards of very articulate cockney children from Camberwell burst in for what was known in those days by the rather blatantly patronising title of Mission Day.

It was amazing to stand by the gate and see the chirping flock swoop down upon us. In those days of great poverty it was almost an economic urgency to 'have a Lady' as we benefactresses were called. Those who had already established contact by letter rushed round saying, 'Are you my Lady, are you my Lady', while those without a shepherd capered like spring lambs seizing any hand they saw free and murmuring insinuatingly, 'Will you be my Lady?'

Once you were hooked there was no escape for the rest of the day and the insatiable appetite of your protégé for any kind of entertainment, since this was for many their one and only day out from the brick walls of South East London, was quite terrifying.

The only time during the day that you had to relax and try to think of further activities to keep up your reputation for entertainment was when you delivered your protégé to one of the many long tables laid out under the Tulip Tree and their boundless energies were directed to the intake of large quantities of food, which temporarily checked their inexhaustible capacity for asking questions.

Of course there were all sorts of play centres, and also casualty clearing stations. There were endless rides on the lake in boats under supervision, but in spite of this quite a few fell in, in their exuberance, but were always rescued. One of these children, when taken to the casualty station for dry clothes, proved to have on eleven jerseys that had all to be peeled off first. Lack of money to buy warm overcoats and lack of fuel in the home, all these deficiencies created the habit of donning as many garments as possible and even keeping them on in midsummer if going to the great open spaces of the countryside which seemed so remote to poor families in those days.

When evening came on we would watch thankfully the great cavalcade form up at the gate ready to move off to the station, like a lot of chickens finding their roosting places when evening approached. When the word to march was given, as the flock sped away we would turn back exhausted, wondering at the vitality and hunger for experience of the children in this vastly different world to ours between which a bridge had been built for this one day.

It was, I suppose, because of these glimpses of it through the eyes of Father Jellicoe and this memorable day that I decided in later years to train as a social worker. But that is a chapter of my later life.

XVIII

Local Ghosts

Apart from our parties at Aunt Mo's, our social life was very much centred round the small town of Cheadle, a few miles away from my father's parish. It was an invigorating bicycle ride there beginning on the rough road that ran past our house along a windy ridge. At the cross roads you turned left and drifted downhill effortlessly on a more civilised asphalt surface, gliding easily in a series of delicious bends, revealing here and there pleasant views across the valley.

After climbing up again on the other side of the valley you entered the town by a road which was flanked by stone walls terracing the hillside. Here some of the bigger houses stood above the road half hidden by plantations of trees. There were sycamores and elms, with the gaps filled in by ornamental rhododendrons, mingling with the polished austerity of copper beeches, so popular then and typical of the brown varnished interiors of Edwardian homes.

In the centre of the town the houses were built of small red brick flanking each street very tall and austere, but their severity was somehow invigorating, it suited this northern setting. Those above the main streets ran across the hillside at strange angles forming attractively individual groups and with roofs providing sharp silhouettes above.

There were two Churches, the Anglican one was built in Georgian style of heavy grey stone, you reached it by a long line of steps leading up from a raised pavement which was also above the road. It was *not* a place anyone would run into easily for a few moments' prayer.

The vicar, a kindly Evangelical, was the son of a peer, and his wife, though fundamentally kind, had acquired something of the Proudie hustle about her, perhaps through some reflected glory from the peerage and was known as 'The Power Behind the Throne'.

Opposite the Church was a beautiful half-timbered building, one of the oldest in the town, which was unspoilt by any restoration. The ground floor was occupied by a saddler. You stepped into it by two well worn steps and were at once in almost semi-darkness. The low oak beamed ceiling was black with age and the air heavy with the smell of leather.

Next to this stood a house of grey stucco, heavily restored but very ancient foundations. It was called Cumberland House because the Duke of Cumberland had slept there before he turned his army north in pursuit of Bonnie Prince Charlie, an excursion that ended in the Battle of Culloden. It was occupied by a great friend of ours, a local personality known to everyone as 'Auntie Cull'. She had rather a florid complexion and intense blue eyes which seemed to enlarge in size as she retailed in a deep voice the local ghost stories of which she was a connoisseur.

There had been some strange happenings even in Cumberland House. She used to tell a story about how she was making the bed one day when the front door bell rang and she went down to speak to a caller.

When she returned to finish it the sheets had been taken off the bed by some unseen hand and coiled up into a tight knot. As the house was empty except for herself, there seemed no other explanation than that of a supernatural one.

The neighbourhood seemed very full of ghost stories, and Auntie Cull was an expert at retailing them with a sense of natural drama. There were many old houses in the surrounding countryside that evidently had good psychic conditions. There was a beautiful Carolinian one, Hales Hall for instance, a few miles out of Cheadle, with a long drive at the side flanked by an avenue of high trees. The house had a charming front with a sharply sloping roof topped by small turreted windows with leaded edges protruding from them. It was a kindly house, with a rather Jane Austen atmosphere about it.

In front of it ran a stretch of water. This was not an innocent ornamental lake of Capability Brown, but a long stretch made sinister by a fringe of yews like an edging of mourners' crepe. It spoke of mysterious tragedy.

Auntie Cull had actually seen a ghost herself there. One evening following the narrow winding road which led up to the drive gate, she had seen a pale woman with a baby wrapped tightly in her arms slip quickly across the road and vanish into the hedge as she looked at her.

It was said that someone fishing there had pulled a woman's body up from the weeds. Whether these two events had any connection with one another we never discovered, unfortunately.

There was a story of the phantom coach, too, which ran along that road. Auntie Cull had not encountered this herself, but she had met the old coachman who had. It could be heard plainly tearing along the quiet country road, and up the drive with clattering hooves, panting horses and harness jingling. As soon as it reached the front door the sound ceased utterly.

The story apparently behind this event was that a past owner of the house had gone up to London in his own coach but on the way back it had been attacked by highwaymen. He never returned home again for he had been shot dead.

It is very difficult to understand why some strange vibration of unfulfilled thought should be operating through the centuries, reiterating perhaps the last frantic dash of the squire's coach to escape attack, linked with a kind of wishful thinking to reach the safety of his drive, a place he never in reality saw in his earthly life again.

Because Auntie Cull was interested in ghost stories she invited confidences about strange happenings from people. There was an old lady living near this Carolian house, Hales Hall, who told her of a very strange and tragic happening in the family. Her eldest son on leaving school took his first job in a small mine which stood in the trees behind this haunted house at a place called Woodhead. He came to his mother one day and said that he was very puzzled because every morning when he got over a certain stile, a lady dressed in black met him and accompanied him to the mine and then vanished. He did not feel apparently that she was an evil presence but he realised that she was something supernatural.

The mother was worried about this. She thought it might be a warning of some sort, so she agreed to accompany the boy to work next day. Unfortunately when the day came she was very busy – it was Monday and wash day and she had the rest of the family to look after – so she told the boy she would go with him the next day.

He went to work alone, and that morning the mine blew up and all the workers were killed. All through her long life the mother had carried this regret that she had not followed her first impression, and accompanied him on that fatal Monday morning. Would she have found out something from the mysterious lady in black, which would have caused her to keep him back from work that day?

It is interesting to ponder on how far this was a psychic happening which might have been utilised to avert disaster, proving that the future is not fixed. If only she had regarded the happening in the same way as St Joseph who 'Being warned of God in a dream went another way', and by the flight into Egypt saved the life of the Christ child.

In later years Auntie Cull was left a widow and moved from the more solemn grandeur of Cumberland House to a much tinier house, a lodge that stood at someone's front gate. It was round like a beehive, the kind of house you would find in a children's fairy story. Her clothes looked a little shabby sometimes and it was rumoured that she was rather poorer than before. But she did not in the least lose prestige, but gained it. Her life did not depend on such superciliousness as 'living up to the Joneses'. In this cosy retreat of old age she became even more of a personality. She continued there till the end of her life dispensing tea in some exquisite cups left her by her grandmother, and continuing her repertoire of ghost stories, to everybody's delight.

I still remember how her large blue eyes used to dilate and her voice grow deeper and more dramatic as she related the favourite of her repertoire. The story of the headless man seen up at the Shaw and how the farmer's wife had exclaimed: 'And, Mrs Cull, never the head of that man did I see!'

It was inevitable that in this small town atmosphere class distinctions should be sharp and social pressures wielded somewhat heavily by certain long established families. Such were a professional family who lived appropriately high up on a walled site nestling among copperbeeches and rhododendrons as you entered the town.

But a similar firmness of spirit characterised the widow of the local draper's family, Mrs Blodwin.

It was perhaps typical of her practical outlook and resistance to class pressures that after having made a modest fortune out of the shop, the family did not immediately become the owners of a country mansion, and forget their commercial enterprise entirely, but turned the shop into a private house clothing the bow window with discreet lace curtains. Behind these, if you peered very hard, you could just see the son of the house, known perpetually as 'young Blodwin' in spite of having reached the stage of greying hair (probably because at the age of 50 he was still an eligible bachelor and a man of substance). Then he would sit in an easy chair placed exactly where bales of material and ladies underwear had once stood, and from this vantage point watch the local inhabitants whom he had once served.

The outstanding personality in the family, however, was Mrs Blodwin, she was small and wiry and bore herself with considerable dignity. She had a very lined face, with white hair drawn back smoothly under a cap of crisp goffered frills. She was possessed of a quick natural intelligence and a great sense of humour.

The story went that old Mrs Blodwin attended a committee meeting, presided over by the ruling monarchs' eldest daughter, who had just returned to the town after her honeymoon, in a welter of congratulations. As the meeting proceeded, guided by the bride's able but ruling hand, her father felt moved to remark to Mrs Blodwin in an indiscreet moment, 'A very wonderful woman my daughter Mrs Chasefield.' To his amazement he got no reply. Thinking she had not heard, he repeated the remark, 'A very wonderful woman my daughter Mrs Chasefield.' A statement which was again received in complete silence. Then becoming irritated by the lack of response to this question to which he felt so convinced there could be only one reply, he boomed out for all to hear,

'A very wonderful woman my daughter Mrs Chasefield.'

Mrs Blodwin's mob cap inclined ever so little towards him, as an acknowledgement of his presence like raising the hat.

Then without a flutter of a goffered frill, came to reply in her clear voice that reached all at the Committee table.

'I fail to see it.'

Such a reply was unheard of and from a draper's wife! The result was something akin to a bomb explosion in the local monarch's vicinity. As he was not altogether beloved even by his so-called friends, they all enjoyed the joke against him, and it was told for a long time.

Years afterwards I met the two grandsons of this ruling power. They were both in high positions, one in the international and academic world and the other in world communications. I found them both likeable people, reasonably adapted to the vast community in which they moved. It was then that I came to see how much of the aggressiveness of the Victorian personality was caused by the geographical limitations of the community then.

In the modern world which knows no local or national boundaries, the family's intelligence and force of character had found expression where they were no longer grotesquely outsize for the community they operated in.

As time went on, we widened our circle of friends still further. In spite of the fact that both my brother and I were self-conscious and socially shy we received innumerable invitations out and were made welcome wherever we went. I think we were lucky in finding among our neighbours people who had something of the same set of values as our own. Social slickness and showmanship meant nothing to them.

While at school I was having the experience of being outside the community around me, at home the very opposite was happening. I was slowly becoming integrated into a social group, for we were lucky in being part of a whole generation of young people who were growing up in the neighbourhood at that time, the children of professional people mostly, like ourselves. We had a common background but sufficient diversity of character and upbringing to give some life to the group, which seemed to form itself in some spontaneous way built round the family of a retired naval officer who lived near Cheadle.

Motivated by a tremendous appetite for life which characterises most healthy young people at that age, we went about everywhere together. No longer did I feel shy and alone when entering a room for some social function. There were always some of these particular friends waiting for me who had inevitably flocked together, and begun exchanging ideas.

One of our hostesses who owned the house where they saw the phantom coach christened us 'The Souls'. I hope we were not cliquy or exclusive as the original ones were. We were certainly not superior or standoffish, most of us were very aware of and interested in the problems of the welfare of the wider community. But because of this personal concern, we needed the smaller group too, for self-expression. Our activities were very varied, from playing tennis on lawns set in old world gardens to tobogganing or skating by moonlight in cold, stone wall country on the Derbyshire side of the county. What a sense of fun and friendliness I found in all these activities.

Within this group, however, I remained the shy, self-conscious schoolgirl, unable to talk freely, and continually missing my cue if something interesting came into my head about the subjects they were talking about. I realise now how much I owe to my friends who accepted me without criticism or pity, and let me enter into the enormous amount of perhaps unsophisticated fun we enjoyed.

I recently read an article by a psychiatrist about the mass emotion generated in teenagers at performances by famous pop singers. He explained how their frantic desire to even touch their heroes' coat-tails during this orgy of emotion demonstrates a very normal urge to belong to a group – to be 'in something'. This, the psychiatrist stated, was really a very harmless outlet for the emotions of the young, which later becomes personified in love for a particular boyfriend, entirely stabilising the situation generally. This explanation and my own experiences has helped me to understand these young people of today.

It would be impossible to speak of all the members of The Souls in person, but suffice it to mention this one large family because they were, I think, the centre round which The Souls revolved, and also because, by some strange plan of fate, they were to open ways for me, to bring to my knowledge certain things which were to be important. This, I have grown to think, is a most valuable function of certain friends you make on the way through life. I have come to the conclusion that there is a plan for us. Quite constantly, the same friends will, often unbeknown to themselves, set part of it in motion for us.

The family lived in a delightful old Georgian house called Thornbury on the fringe of Auntie Cull's ghost story country where there were many remarkably old houses. As far as I know, Thornbury had no ghost. Certainly there was nothing sinister about it. It was a particularly sunny, friendly sort of house, standing high up with a scattering of tall trees behind it, just enough to give it dignity without shutting it in.

Its inside was comfortable in a very friendly way. Their father Commander Anstey was a retired naval commander, who prior to coming to Thornbury had been lent to the Chilean Navy. In consequence of this, the family spoke Spanish, and had a wider horizon than those of us who had lived in the district all our lives.

They could act well and read most of the important books which came out, and discussed them easily. They were also informed in Church matters, one half choosing to go to the local church presided over by our good friend the Irish rural dean, and the rest walking miles, often fasting, in order to attend a very high Anglican Church under the direction of a priest called Father Alexander. Their differing tastes were accepted most amicably in the family, in fact they invented a delicious parody to describe them, which began, 'Some talk of Alexander and some of Gibbons Payne.' It went well to the rousing tune of the British Grenadiers.

They, too, had a family vocabulary, much as we did. For instance, when telling any stories about their neighbours, they would always say in a discreet voice, 'speaking in all L and C', i.e. love and charity. Needless to say, in spite of this apparent sarcasm, they were seldom unkind in their comment, though often very witty.

Hugh, the youngest brother, who had a rather dramatic, impelling style, being a good amateur actor, used to pause after his best stories, and then remark loudly, 'Ah, ha, I thought that would shake you!'

As if to make a complete trilogy of religious views in the house, their American stepmother was a Christian Scientist.

They always had governesses for the three step-children of the mother's persuasion.

Unfortunately, they constantly seemed to have acute appendicitis soon after they took the post. In those days before antibiotics were invented, this illness caused great anxiety for it could very easily prove fatal if left too long. An awful battle then began between those in favour of the doctor being called and those not. After preliminary skirmishings however, the Commander, who was a charming, quiet man, firmly took over the command of the family ship, and steered it safely into port by having the governess rapidly removed to hospital and operated on, after which she invariably recovered.

The three small boys, brought up in this mixed theological group, naturally developed enquiring minds in theological matters. There was the story of how they were caught having a spitting match – who could spit furthest – and were put in the corner as a punishment. After a while the eldest one, Richard, looked round and remarked in injured tones to his governess, 'Miss Moore, Jesus spat,' a theological assertion which it was difficult to deal with.

On another occasion, the boys asked what a miracle was, and Miss Moore replied, 'Well, Jesus turned water into wine.' At which Christopher Robin replied gleefully in a lisping voice, 'Yesh, and I turned my bathing suit into pyjamas.' Appropriately enough, Christopher Robin became in later years the head of a famous theological college.

In spite of their separate life in the nursery, common in those days to most children from the middle classes upwards, they had quite a sense of participation in adult life. When their elder step-sister, Ruth, got married, they very much enjoyed her wedding reception, but during the function approached the bride with very puzzled countenances.

'Did Daddy and Mummy have a lovely party like this when they were married?' Richard said.

'Oh yes,' remarked their step-sister, 'a very lovely big one in London.'

'Then why,' asked Richard indignantly, 'were we not invited?'

That wedding was another landmark, for I was asked to be a bridesmaid for the first time in my life by my very kind namesake, Ruth, who had always been a source of sympathy and help to all of us. It was marvellous to feel you had some designated position, but with no alarming responsibilities and were not just one of a crowd.

I can remember the culmination of the event, when, dressed in beige lace, we sat out in the rock garden, amid the wafting scents of a warm June day, and had our photos taken poised on the rocks, among the clinging fronds of the rock plants.

I little thought then that the bride and I would not meet again for 25 years, when she would return from Kenya with two grown-up daughters. Yet she seemed much the same person, sympathetically concerned about the practical problems of everybody in either land.

Ursula, the youngest of the family, was in many ways the most mature. She had sparkling violet eyes, and a quick repartee which always caused her to engage in animated conversation, which appeared to me even flirtatious, with many members of the opposite sex, from benevolent clerics like the Vicar, who had a ready Irish wit, to boys of her own age. Her sophistication seemed quite amazing to me in those days, considering she was still at school. She would appear, for instance, at a local dance with the air of a mature woman, clad in an elegant long frock and then roll it up, to people's alarm, and take her handkerchief out of her stocking top like any schoolgirl.

Later on, when she left a strict academic domain, designed chiefly for the daughters of the clergy, she took Social Science at the School of Economics, and became an ardent Socialist.

This was something that seemed staggering to us in our quiet backwater. The pros and cons of the competing political parties never entered into our lives, for everyone other than the industrial working class, became automatically a Conservative. In those days I had never even heard of the Fabians, and the famous Socialist intellectuals, except Bernard Shaw. I recall with amusement now our suppressed horror at her action, and my secret admiration also, at her daring.

Another cause for surprise, but in this case unbridled admiration, was her action in becoming a social worker when she was so smart and sophisticated. I had always thought of them in terms of the bossy old-fashioned ladies, who busied themselves over the affairs of the diocese, striding forth to pursue so-called good works relentlessly.

Such people had already created another conflict and frustration in my life, for, brought up as I was in a Vicarage where service to the community was so emphasised, I longed to be active in such work, but felt completely in rebellion against such personnel. Ursula and her course were to be yet another landmark on my road, to indicate the way to bring two divergent points together, and show me the path I was later to follow by becoming a student of LSE myself.

My social activity with The Souls even extended finally into the dreaded world of dancing. Since I was now the member of a particular group, I did not want for partners, and began to lose some of my dread of such events. I discovered that I was light on my feet, and when not harassed by a regimented memorising of steps like the dancing class, I could follow my partner intuitively, and do rather well.

Our doctor at Cheadle, who gave the party every year on Christmas Day, now began to arrange at Easter a fancy dress dance in the local town hall. My mother, in one of those sudden outbursts of extravagance to which she appeared subject owing to her richer, middle class upbringing in earlier years, wrote to Gamages and hired two fancy dresses for us. As far as I can recall, they were more her choice than ours, but I don't think this worried us. For my brother she got a barrister's wig and gown, which I must say rather suited his bespectacled dignity.

My mother chose for me a grey Quaker costume, with a stiff white collar and cap. The demureness of it suited my modest approach to life in those days, though I feel on looking back that I should really have taken the opportunity to come out in something extremely flamboyant to express some hidden quality in my make-up which I had not had the chance to use before. It was strange my mother should choose a Quaker dress, however, in view of the close connection I was to have with The Society of Friends later. I don't recall in those days envisaging them as anything but a strange sect which Nanny used to tell a funny story about. It was something to do with an old lady sitting waiting for the spirit to move her. I imagined they had faded out of modern life as completely as the costume I wore on this special occasion. It was a pity someone did not inform me about them, for had I met them earlier, I might have been launched into a whole new vista of friends and valuable ideas which only came to me much later in life.

By the time the Fancy Dress Ball was held the next year, the group consciousness of The Souls had grown so considerably that we essayed to go collectively as one huge centipede. To avoid the difficulty of members of both sexes entering a cloakroom in order to don 'the costume', we 'robed' at a doctor's house opposite the town hall. Members of the group had made the costume out of old sheets, and had painted strange marks like ribs on it in black and yellow, giving it a waspish appearance. When inside, we walked in a cramped position with our hands on the hips of the person in front of us. Only our legs were showing, and on these we all wore long black stockings, to be in unison and look as much like some strange creeping creature as possible.

The traffic in those days was very slight, so we did not have any police escort in order to cross the High Street. When we were all lined up inside this extraordinary vehicle, we moved off down the drive and across the public highway which was rather wide there owing to a junction of roads, but luckily no vehicle appeared to cut us in half. Luckily, it was early in the evening, for some perfectly self-respecting client issuing from 'The White Horse' on the corner might well have questioned his sobriety had he suddenly come upon us, and feared that he had entered on the advanced stages of D.T.

Our arrival at the main entrance did not go unnoticed, however, for in those days the surplus population could not sit cosily at home viewing the whole world on the changing face of a television screen. Starved therefore, of visual entertainment, no local event of any import passed their notice, and as soon as the time drew near for its commencement, a restless crowd would be seen lining the main entrance, hungry for entertainment. On this occasion, of course, they were the recipients of a real feast of visual food. As we gathered from the sounds audible even inside the precincts of the 'vehicle', the arrival of this monstrosity caused extreme hilarity and comment. This would not have worried us had not the younger and more inarticulate members of the crowd expressed their feelings by giving heavy pinches to each of the long, black excrescences of legs as they passed them by.

I do not recall if after this marathon we were accorded a prize. Again, like the cloakroom problem, the mixing of the sexes probably occasioned some difficulty regarding classification. It must have been hard for the judges to decide whether we should be awarded a prize as a first-class lady or gentleman.

It was out of this rather pedestrian activity that our local dance club sprang up. We used to meet once a month in some smaller rooms above the town hall, and foxtrot sentimentally to the latest tunes played on a gramophone. That instrument had now passed out of the stage of the large tulip-coloured gramophone with a horn we knew in the nursery, and achieved the status of a discreet brown cabinet, with fluted shutters from which the sound issued forth, the forerunner of the radiogram.

A new addition to our group on these dance occasions was the sisters Frost. Their descriptive name was portrayed clearly in their appearance. They sparkled tantalisingly, yet with just that pale chill of whiteness that lies behind that phenomenon on a crisp morning. The fluffier of the two appeared to be a great success with Hugh, the younger of the brothers from Thornbury whom I secretly admired. When they drifted off together on to the dance floor (and they were usually the first couple to begin), she in her pastel crepe de chine and ciro pearls, leaving a smell of delicate perfume in her wake, I felt jealous and frustrated. I was still allied to the heavy brogued woman of the blue-stocking variety through home and school, who generally married professors or parsons, and based their unions on intellectual equality. Clearly it did not pay in social life to be a woman of ideas, I felt, as I watched Miss Frost, clinging so gently yet tenaciously to Hugh, like her namesake does on gates and branches in the early morning.

Because I was not individually a social success, or the sort of girl who got 'dated' often by men, I began to be the one who ran things. This is, of course, always a good role for the socially unsuccessful.

I organised a film club among other things and we bought a cine camera, but our efforts to enact what in those days were considered dramatic episodes of the films proved rather a failure.

A huge snowball which we tried to push down hill and wreck a car driving up to Thornbury broke into harmless fragments just as it landed in front of it.

We did some of our filming in the most delightful old house, The Lodge, situated on the side of a hill. It was the home of another member of the Souls, a doctor's son called Peter Bearblock, whose special hobby was vintage cars. This was another very hospitable, easy-going house presided over by Peter's delightful parents known to most of us as Aunt Bonnie and Uncle Peter. It had some rather unusual features – a house of character, the agents would have called it. For instance, if you went into the entrance hall, a kind of sitting room full of antique furniture, and walked up the wide stairs, you were amazed to find that one door led into the doctor's surgery and then out into the back yard among Peter's vintage cars. The gradient of the hillside was so steep. Of course, the bedrooms were all up there too. I recall staying a night there sometimes. My mother and I were given the big guest room and I retired to bed in a wonderful old double bed with a huge canopy with side curtains, the room lit by the soft light of a real fire in the old iron grate.

We were just settling for sleep in this idyllic atmosphere, which seemed far away from the contingencies of modern war when there was a sudden thump, the door burst open and the sash window fell right down at the top, and the whole grate fell out of the wall on to the floor – mantelpiece and all!

We were so convulsed with laughter at this episode that we could hardly lift the grate up at first. The old mantelpiece was very heavy.

Our filming took place on a huge covered verandah at the side of the sitting room on the lower floor which had the appearance of a room for the limited area of a camera. The idea was that the heroine should be shut in there, overcome with some visible type of gas, and the hero should break in and rescue her in the nick of time.

To give the effect of this danger a friend standing by offered to light his pipe and puff smoke across the lens of the camera, to look like gas. This appeared to go beautifully until the picture was developed. We then discovered that the whole scene including the pipe and smoker were reflected in the large sash window at the back of the verandah and showed clearly on the film.

After this we removed to the less complicated scenery of a hillside covered with scrub somewhere on the way to Buxton. But even in these breezy open heights complications ensued. We planned another most exciting rescue scene, the heroine on this occasion being a very charming French girl who was a member of the group Simmone. She agreed to be rescued from rascals by a stalwart hero and carried by him screaming and with suitable emotional gestures down the hillside. But unfortunately this solid young Englishman, while eminently suitable for carrying heavy weights, was not equally agile and he tripped over a bush at the critical moment when the chase was really on and deposited the heroine in a rabbit hole. As we were not intending to act professionally we gave up the club after that.

XIX

Cross-Currents in the Family

This inability to express myself, especially to communicate with the opposite sex even in our friendly group, made me, I suppose, even more dependent on my family, and brought to light some psychological problems that had begun many years back in our earlier lives.

The resentment and frustration that had made me burst through the baize doors into the hall as a small child exclaiming, 'What a beast of a brother I've got!' had not diminished with the years. In fact, it had gained somewhat in importance. In spite of going to the same kind of school as my brother, I had never really caught up on him in education or interests. Now that he was an undergraduate at Oxford, and I was only a leggy schoolgirl, we seemed to belong to different worlds. When he brought his medical student friends home he liked to play singles with them on the tennis court. He never asked me to join him. I don't recall that we even met at tea.

My girl friends were not his type either. Mildred I found rather difficult to communicate with; her quiet poise embarrassed me because it was such a contrast to my own uncertainty covered up by boisterousness. I suppose I was too shy then to embark on the task of trying to get to know her better as I did much later when she became a much beloved nun. The two friends I made, Bea and Muriel, who were her neighbours were less complex. They had all the characteristics of the feminine and we talked chiefly of fashions and local gossip. They came from that local mecca, the Five Towns and always wore very pretty clothes.

My emotional state over this situation seemed to reach rather a climax before a picnic I went on with them. My mother had bought me a particularly smart brown and beige coat, made in a two-tone boucle, a material very fashionable in those days. I was determined to wear it on this occasion, but my mother felt it was too fragile for such an outing. She advocated my school coat of blue serge.

I no longer had any burning desire to wear this garment, as I used to. The mass opinion against such clothes had killed the pride I had felt in the uniform of a famous school. I was beginning to emerge now as a self-conscious individual. I wanted to look my best at all times.

My mother became adamant on the matter. I recall, in my fury and frustration, standing on the study hearth and kicking the kerb until some of the tiles fell out. This was a very undignified proceeding at my age and caused much surprise, but I think on the whole I felt better for it and made me understand vandalism.

I remember my brother remonstrated with my mother for not bringing me up with more firm discipline – I secretly agreed with him because I felt I could have appreciated his logical, consistent reasoning in the matter. My mother, having the more feminine approach, was indulgent in some things, and then adamant in others. If only she could have realised how much clothes meant to me, and the effect they had on my whole personality at that age. Ever since the bicycle rides to parties in my pleated skirt and jersey I had had a sense of inferiority and eccentricity regarding my clothes in comparison to other girls. I remember my mother chiding me over my anxiety, and citing Josephine, a friend who was very independent and always landed on her feet in school, as one who never felt like this. I tried to explain what I knew inwardly, that her assurance and independent character made her success in impressing people so that outward apparel was less important to her.

I cannot recall whether I won the battle to wear the coat or not, but I know I went on the picnic, for I have some photos of my friends standing by the car near a beautiful old Abbey we visited called Croxden, down winding lanes somewhere in the damson orchards near Denstone. In those days it was singularly unspoilt, and I recall the fascinating medieval atmosphere in the ruins, and the complete rural peace round the houses near to them. That memory has proved more lasting than the clothes I went there in, though at the time the clothes seemed all important.

Through this episode I felt I had lost some social standing, as it were, in the family and further justified my brother's estimate that I was just an immature schoolgirl, not suitable to admit to his more adult manly circle. And yet I had done it to keep up my prestige among my girl friends and anyone else I met when with them. How difficult it was to reconcile the two worlds.

This kind of situation also brought out the great difference between my mother's and my own way of life, which developed through my going to a large public school. My mother had been educated at a small private school devoutly evangelical in a Midland town quite near us. She could not understand the larger, tougher environment into which I had been precipitated, and the need to protect oneself with apparent hardness and independence.

There were, I realise now, other reasons for this defence mechanism, due to a psychological problem in our family, the significance of which I could only realise in more mature years.

My mother idolised my brother, and loved him in a way she could never love me. Knowing what I do now about the possibilities of reincarnation, it may have been partly because they had been husband and wife in another life. But this relationship was also due to the frustrations of her own married life. My grandmother had brought her up in complete innocence of the facts of life. She was not even allowed to read the newspaper in her early twenties for fear she saw something in it that 'was not nice'. She married without having the slightest idea of the details of physical marriage.

She used to recall how, during her engaged days, Granny once found her sitting in the drawing room in the twilight with her very respectable clergyman friend, Granny was so shocked that she made my mother feel she had done something very wicked, though how or why my mother had no idea.

Much to the family's surprise, my mother's friendship with George Plant did ripen into an engagement and, apparently quite unprepared, my mother set out on the road to marriage. She always told me how terribly embarrassed she felt when

Daddy showed her the letter he had written to the Raven Hotel at Shrewsbury, asking for a double room for the first night of their honeymoon. The idea that she had to share a room with a man she had been criticised for sitting in the twilight with filled her with a sense of horror – this indeed was impropriety!

When Daddy kissed her in the carriage going home from the church, she found it quite impossible to unbend, even to a man she loved, so rigid had her Victorian upbringing made her.

I think she was happier the second day of their marriage, for she used to tell an amusing story of how they awoke at the little pub at Llanaghrig, the highest village in Wales, and saw Daddy's old friend, Thomas ab Griffith the road man, under the bedroom window. Hearing of the arrival of the happy couple, he had most conveniently arranged to do the road exactly outside the hotel in order not to miss them the moment they descended to breakfast.

My father had met Thomas ab Griffith in a pub during the first of his many visits to the village. (The old man adhered so much to the traditional way of life that he used the ancient prefix 'ab' meaning son of.) He was obviously mystified by my father's presence, sensing he was not one of the local Welsh clergymen. After eyeing him for some time, his curiosity overcame him, and leaning forward, said in husky tones, 'Vicar here?' My father smiled, and shook his head, loth to disperse the air of mystery the old man seemed to sense. Then he moved nearer, and murmured confidentially over his mug of beer, 'Someut a preachin?' My father again shook his head. Finally, he communicated to him the reason for his visit. When Griffith found that my father so loved Wales that he came all the way from England regularly for holidays there, he was very delighted, and accepted him as a life-long friend.

On this first morning of their honeymoon, when Griffith had made the acquaintance of the bride, he remarked with great solemnity to my father, 'You're all right, but she's a nicer lady than you are.'

'But then,' remarked my father, greatly appreciating the joke, 'I don't happen to be a lady, Griffith.'

After that, he went away to cogitate over his turf cuttings, while my mother and father climbed the hills to carry out one of the tasks of their honeymoon, searching for Daddy's favourite beagle, Stella, who had gone wild, and was living on the mountains somewhere there. Actually, they did not find her themselves, but later on someone else did. She came back to them safe and sound, and as fat as butter (having lived on rabbits, I suppose), after 16 weeks of freedom. Most surprisingly, she settled down quite happily again in the quiet domestic life at the Vicarage. Like her master, I suppose she revelled in Welsh holidays in the open air.

In this latter activity, my father and mother had a deep bond. There was nothing too hard for my mother to do, walking or sitting by the river while he fished. She always said it was there she learnt the wonderful warmth provided by newspapers tucked inside the coat when inactivity proved chilling in an icy wind. Often they would ride home from Wales on their bicycles as much as 80 miles in a day in order to get back to the parish on the date they had promised.

It was wonderful that my mother succeeded in adjusting herself to the very different tempo of the Plant family. Perhaps she was thankful to get away from its punctual formalism. She used to recall with great amusement how Daddy would drag her into the last carriage of a train just as it moved out, and sink thankfully on a seat, remarking, 'Just nice time, as your dear mother would say.' This was an allusion to the fact that my grandmother always arrived downstairs immaculately attired in her bonnet at least one hour before the carriage was due at the door.

My father and I had much in common, but there was a very great barrier to communication with him. He was terribly deaf, and this handicapped all the little day to day conversations and comments en passant in the rush of life which were possible with Mummy. Only if you sat down and made a special effort to talk could you really carry on a consecutive conversation with Daddy, and being very hard-working, he was out much of the day in the parish.

I loved him and all his family for their warm, easy-going nature, their zest for life, and their capacity for practical jokes. This was underlined with a deep concern and sympathy for their neighbours and an open friendliness.

Sometimes I contrasted it unnecessarily bitterly with my mother's family, who placed so much importance on an orderly way of life, and family possessions, as an essential to peace of mind and comfort. This hurt my mother because they had a great sense of responsibility within the family, and were very liberal to us personally as relations.

My father shared my love of poetry, which was very important, because none of my friends at that time seemed to do so. But we did not belong to the same generation. We had very different tastes, and it was difficult through his deafness, to discuss the subtleties of these things. He loved Tennyson, and I loved Rupert Brooke. I recall once that he read me some verses from 'In Memoriam', his favourite poem, and I followed this by reading some lines from 'Grantchester'. The differences of tone and rhythm quite appalled me. It was rather like listening to a vast philharmonic orchestra followed by chamber music, I suppose.

Nothing could, however, cause me to lose my love of Rupert Brooke. He had become a pillar in my philosophy of life, an impetus for living, which I could not dispense with. In his works, I had found the idea of the heroic, the sense of dedication in war transferred from the stories in the children's book to the more mature medium of poetry. How I read again and again that sonnet,

> Now, God be thanked Who has matched us with His hour,
>   And caught our youth, and wakened us from sleeping,
> With hand made sure, clear eye, and sharpened power,
>   To turn, as swimmers into cleanness leaping ...

I little knew that when I reached my fifties I should be marching with the youth of a new generation, on the long road from Aldermaston, united with them against the very thing that I so idealised now, seeking the preservation of peace and security in the world grown weary of the false ideals of war. How strangely naive our outlook came to seem in the light of the atomic age.

It was good, perhaps, that my belief in the heroic image in poetry was not undermined at that time, for it was to support me through some bad storms first. Some people would call it as a form of escape, but I would say that I rather had to transfer their philosophy to the vaster horizon from which they reflected the real and eternal truth.

Among the poems I came to know and love in that wartime generation, so ably collected by J.C. Squire later, was the one written by Maurice Baring in memory of Julian Grenfell:

> Because of you we will be glad and gay,
> Remembering you, we will be brave and strong.

How true I still feel that more simple utterance to be since I have become more aware of the nearness of the unseen, the triumph of the dead over death.

My brother had a love of poetry too, but his was a more personal relationship, I think. His favourite poet was Swinburne, he would often repeat those verses from 'The Triumph of Time';

> There lived a singer in France of old
> By the tideless dolorous midland sea.
> In a land of sand and ruin and gold
> There shone one woman, and none but she.
> And finding life for her love's sake fail,
> Being fain to see her, he bade set sail,
> Touched land, and saw her as life grew cold,
> And praised God, seeing: and so died he.

The classical foundations of his education seemed to have given him a certain dignity and poise which was far beyond my reach. I used to get very irritable both with my mother and Ralph.

The most annoying factor in this situation was my brother's complete immunity to my irritation, so that I found absolutely no opportunity to 'let off steam' through having a quarrel with him. He was not in the least self-righteous or smug about it. I suppose he had the ideal temperament for a doctor. He just looked at me and my storms with a kindly detachment, advising my mother sometimes on how to bring me up. I can recall hitting him, and trying to wrest his book from him when he was lying on the sofa reading Gray's *Anatomy*, or some standard medical work, but he fended off my attack with a smile as he would some voracious puppy, which made me, I suppose, the more frustrated. His manly aloofness seemed unkind to me, though I don't think, on looking back, that he meant it that way.

I did not receive any encouragement or sympathy in my frustration from the world outside the family, for everyone idolised Ralph, from old ladies to children. This quiet, bespectacled young man seemed to have some extraordinary gift of attraction, I realised. When we visited Mildred's cousin in a little cottage near the Grange, the six children ran to him immediately, and swarmed on his bicycle, breaking his glasses in their enthusiasm, but he still remained interested and unperturbed. Old ladies adored him, even those who met him only for a short moment would ask later, 'Who was that young man with the charming manners and smile?'

The red letter day in the family came when he went to see Granny, and after the visit she seized hold of Daddy's clerical coat, and shouted in his ear, 'Ralph is a very charming young man. Tell him to come and see me again.' He was the first object in the family that my grandmother had ever spoken in praise of, and not criticised. We gasped with amazement, and my mother glowed with pride.

In all this admiration, my brother never became 'precious' like many young men do. I realise now, he made some friends of fine calibre. One was to be a world-famous gynaecologist, and the other a beloved general practitioner. I always felt that his friends indicated Ralph's instinct for genius and sincerity. It was these qualities and this way of life which caused the Bursar of Queens to write of him after his death as a student, 'His influence in the College was powerful for good.'

XX

Nanny Moves to the Lawn

My brother always retained his great affection for Nanny that he had shown as a child, and often bicycled over to visit her in her home. Only recently I came across his long and very carefully written letter to her after her mother died, suggesting she should consider the possibility of coming back to live with us at Dilhorne again and making her very welcome if she did.

But though she had to leave her first home, Hurst Cottage, Nanny never left her own neighbourhood again. She did not feel happy in the bleak winters in North Staffordshire among the coal pits and the smoky slag heaps. The boisterous mining community were somewhat alien to her. She belonged to the quiet pastoral lands of the borders of Staffordshire and Shropshire and the country folk there in spite of the years she had spent away.

When she left Hurst Cottage she went first to live on what they called 'The Lawn'. The modern dictionary terms it 'a plot of grass kept closely mown', but the word goes back further in history than the conventional garden plot and the area of the Blymhill Lawn where Nanny lived included several acres of fields and houses. It was a sort of plateau above the village of Blymhill where Nanny's sister Edie, who had been parlour maid to the famous Auntie Bea now lived, having married a Shropshire farmer.

There was one very pretty farm just after you left the main road, the famous Roman road, Watling Street. But this farm was spoilt for me because according to the notice on the gate, it was also the slaughter house. Next came another farm and then Nanny's cottage. Her house stood some way back from the road and sideways on to it.

I do not recall this home anything like so well as Hurst

Cottage, partly because I had grown older, I suppose, and did not have to be packed off to Nanny's when some crisis occurred. But the house itself did not appear to have the same character and appearance of the former one. It was isolated in fields and was approached by a narrow lane, and although it had a cottage garden, the main factor I recall were the wealth of small bushes round it. If you came out when it was getting dusk and followed the garden path to the toilet at the side of the house, these bushes rustled mysteriously and gave one the feeling that some unseen figure might be lurking in them so that you were always glad to get back into the house.

The chief asset was the new range of walks. There was a lane just across the Watling Street nearly opposite the turning to Nanny's which wound alluringly on. But there were ash trees down near a bend in the lane and the autumn wind in them made the peculiar moaning noise that seemed again to speak of the sorrow in the world that I feared and caused me to make Nanny turn back home.

There were more urban expeditions to the post office at Weston under Lizard on the main road where they kept a delectable kind of biscuit called Custard Creams which Nanny always bought for me and I consumed with great avidity.

Just beyond Nanny's on the way down to the village was Miss Botterill's house. A small one which might be called a cottage, but it was never referred to as that as in those days the fashion for the gentry acquiring cottages had not become fashionable, and Miss Botterill was very much 'the gentry', I always imagine. Strangely enough I never saw her myself but I have a vivid picture of her as she was spoken of with considerable respect by Nanny and the neighbours, and her remarks when on outings noted.

She was to me the very personification of discreet spinsterhood, perhaps on a modest income. I do not know; but the closely clipped hedges which encircled her house in a kind of nest gave her an abundance of that discreet privacy which was an essential attribute of the single lady living on her own in those days and created a fascinating air of mystery.

Soon after you passed her house and the big farm that stood on the edge of the hill, you descended the High Hall Bank, a romantic name it seemed to me somehow linked perhaps in my mind with Tennyson in his poem 'Maud'.

There were many 'Banks' round Nanny's, this being the local and rather expressive name for hill. There was Ivetsey Bank on the Watling Street just by the turn to Nanny's old house and just beyond the turn off to the Lawn was The Wallery Bank. Here Nanny recalled a fearful episode as a child when her sisters had taken her for a walk there and 'tended to leave her' as she described it quoting her childish language. It was indicative of the great security of the village child of that time that this seemed a single threat that stood out in her mind so long. The same cannot be said for many modern children in the more insecure and tense environment of the present day.

Certainly alarm caused by the threat was somewhat justified as local tradition had it that The Wallery had something to do with wolves having been there in the past. Such a happening seemed curiously remote as I remember it because it was flanked by an almost urban grey stone wall behind which stood an area of trees and shrubs which sheltered one of the drives up to the house of the local Earl.

The High Hall Bank led down to the village and the Grange where Nanny's sister lived with her farmer husband and two daughters, Myrtle and Hazel. It was a delightful old house. The garden at the back was full of lupins of vivid blue if you called in June.

The rooms on the left of the front door were very extensive and more than the family required, so they became the centre of guests who were a source of great interest to Nanny. The place was an ideal retreat for spinster ladies of moderate means with 'treasures' like Edie and Nanny to look after them.

Our own Aunt Aggie moved in for a considerable time, bringing her furniture with her. She was my father's favourite sister. She had very blue eyes and was very fond of wearing that colour too. 'Aunt Aggie's blue' as it was called in the family. She had a great enthusiasm for food which rather outstripped her digestive capacities and was famous for her little paper bags in which she carried various 'nibbles' but mostly soda mints to cope with their bad effects. 'Oh Alice,' I recall her remarking to my mother after eating one of the latter's delicious tomato dishes with bread crumbs top flavoured with sugar, 'I feel as if I had swallowed the piano, but never mind, it was worth it!'

She had quite a few little fads which seemed an enigma to those who served her. She must have been a pioneer in food reform I suppose (though we did not recognise it then) for I remember when my mother was pressing her to leave a letter she was writing and come for a walk, she shouted, 'Oh do leave me a minute. I am just inciting Evie to eat carrots!' Evie was another aunt who had been stricken with rheumatism badly.

Aunt Aggie brought to the Grange among other strange paraphernalia a Chair Bed. It was always spoken of as Aunt Aggie's Chair Bed as if no one else ever had one. It was a sort of forerunner of the Studio Couch, I suppose. It had a railed back and arms which made it very limiting in length for a tall person. No let down arms in those days to allow for height. I slept on it many years later in Nanny's last home but by that time it had begun to have some ominous 'sags' in it which were comfortably padded by Nanny's feather bed and helped one to take off a few inches in length by not lying straight out.

Aunt Aggie also brought her piano with her. She was the musical one of the family and sometimes played the organ in Church. She used to play hymns on the piano so beautifully that Aunt Mamie who had married a local curate who had later turned into a Communist, was in agony and called out, 'Stop, stop Aggie, if you play those hymns again you will have me back in the Church of England!'

So Nanny went on serving the family in a way even though she had left our home many years before. Besides this she devoted herself to helping her sister with the domestic problems of the farm and the upbringing of her two nieces.

During all this time she changed very little from the wonderful person we had known, either in nature or appearance.

All her life Nanny remained wedded to the idea of grey or black clothes in unison with her former uniform except for the one interlude of the coloured pinafore. She had explained when I gave her coloured things, that somehow she did not feel right in them after wearing uniform so much of her life. She was a beautiful needlewoman and could have made herself all sorts of gay things.

The lovely smocks and dainty dresses she made for me she never wanted to translate into grown-up editions for herself. But she loved gay colours for her needlework.

Towards the end of her life I obtained for her a varied collection of brightly coloured balls of wool to crochet with. Actually she did not use them all before she died, she was too old.

I had forgotten about these balls so I was very surprised when going to a psychic group to ask about the whereabouts of a lost dog I received instead a message from Nanny through a perfect stranger in the group. 'I see a little old white-haired lady who comes to you with great affection and thanks. She is laying on your knee a pile of balls of brightly coloured wool. She says you did not use them. She did.'

So Nanny, as her self-styled epithet records, is still active in her sewing and perhaps as she suggests mending the angels' breeches; who knows?